utb 5331

D1731213

**Eine Arbeitsgemeinschaft der Verlage**

Böhlau Verlag · Wien · Köln · Weimar
Verlag Barbara Budrich · Opladen · Toronto
facultas · Wien
Wilhelm Fink · Paderborn
Narr Francke Attempto Verlag / expert Verlag · Tübingen
Haupt Verlag · Bern
Verlag Julius Klinkhardt · Bad Heilbrunn
Mohr Siebeck · Tübingen
Ernst Reinhardt Verlag · München
Ferdinand Schöningh · Paderborn
transcript Verlag · Bielefeld
Eugen Ulmer Verlag · Stuttgart
UVK Verlag · München
Vandenhoeck & Ruprecht · Göttingen
Waxmann · Münster · New York
wbv Publikation · Bielefeld

Simone Broders

# **Academic Skills**

## An Introduction for English and American Studies

Wilhelm Fink

*The Author:*
Priv.-Doz. Dr. Simone Broders teaches English Literary and Cultural Studies at the University of Erlangen-Nürnberg. Her particular research interests incorporate the literature of the 'Long' Eighteenth Century, contemporary writing, discourses of knowledge, agnotology, alterity studies, as well as popular culture.

Online offers or electronic editions are available at
**www.utb-shop.de**

Bibliographic information published by the Deutsche Nationalbibliothek

The Deutsche Nationalbibliothek lists this publication in the Deutsche Nationalbibliografie; detailed bibliographic data available online: http://dnb.d-nb.de

© 2020 Wilhelm Fink Verlag, ein Imprint der Brill-Gruppe
(Koninklijke Brill NV, Leiden, Niederlande; Brill USA Inc., Boston MA, USA; Brill Asia Pte Ltd, Singapore; Brill Deutschland GmbH, Paderborn, Deutschland)

Internet: www.fink.de

Cover design: Atelier Reichert, Stuttgart
Production: Brill Deutschland GmbH, Paderborn

UTB Volume number: 5331
ISBN: 978-3-8252-5331-8

# Table of Contents

# Preface: How to Be Curious

It is a truth universally acknowledged that students in possession of a considerable wealth of knowledge must be in want of support with their research papers.

This sentence, loosely based on Jane Austen,[1] seems to gain more and more validity even or especially in the information age. Granted: It has obviously become easier to obtain information on a particular subject. Rarely do students handle a microfiche (let alone a catalogue of index cards) at the library nor do they take involuntary climbing trips on shaky ladders to reach a book on the top shelf. Instead, mobile phones, tablet PCs, and netbooks deliver more sources within seconds at the push of a button than students can use for a 10- to 20-page paper. Spelling and grammar are checked by the word processing programme, the formatting is done by the template once it has been created. With all these tools, it has become easier than ever to write a great academic research paper.

Really? Then the work submitted to universities in recent years should actually have become better and better in the sense of a teleological development and, true to the paradigm of linear progress, strive towards a 'Golden Age of perfect term papers', as it were. Instead, many university teachers complain that the quality of student works is deteriorating, that spelling and expression even in one's own native language are inadequate; the number of plagiarism cases is steadily increasing,[2] as is the number of those who attend several seminars in succession without submitting so much as a single useful paper at the end of the semester. Likewise, students complain about a lack of guidance on how to work independently. How can one develop a new thesis when prac-

---

[1]   Jane Austen, Donald J. Gray (ed.), *Pride and Prejudice*. Norton Critical Edition. The 1813 First Edition Text (New York: Norton, ³2001).

[2]   See chapter 10, this volume.

tically everything has already been written by other, smarter minds?

Obviously, it is not only important to find as much information as possible about a certain problem as quickly as possible. It is more important how this piece of information is understood and critically evaluated, how results from other people's work can be used profitably, and how new theses can be formulated and supported in order to advance one's own research.

Your own research? For many, this is already the core of the problem. Often the composition of a term paper serves primarily for course assessment. Term papers are a necessary evil on the way to graduation. Therefore, no more time and care is spent on their preparation than on any ordinary exam – demonstrating what you have learnt by heart seems to be the main goal, whereas applying one's knowledge, acquiring new skills, and observing good academic practice play a subordinate role. Only a fraction of all students who have submitted a term paper take advantage of having their work supervised by the lecturers during the writing process, or of receiving individual feedback afterwards. Accordingly, students who have not familiarized themselves with the results of their efforts repeatedly make the same mistakes in the coursework of higher semesters as they did in their first proseminar. If you have obtained this practice book to find out how to write an academic paper, first ask yourself two short questions:

## 1) Do you take yourself seriously?

By submitting a term paper, you are not supposed to demonstrate that you can summarize secondary literature and format a text document, but you should enter into a dialogue with other members of the scientific community – these can be other students from your course (often homework is based on papers previously presented in the course) or the teaching staff. Be aware that once you graduate, you may never again have the opportunity to try your hand at researching and to discuss your own findings in an academic environment. Surely, especially if you are at the beginning of your studies, your own research is still in its infancy. This does not mean, however, that you and the results of your research will not be taken seriously. If you deliver an uninspired text in which you ruminate established positions and do not even take the trouble to proofread your manuscript, you prove that you do not take yourself and your work seriously. In that case, you cannot expect others to appreciate your writing.

## 2) Are you curious?

Try to find a topic that arouses your curiosity about a particular aspect of the seminar. As historian Edmund S. Morgan notes, when asked why they are investigating a particular phenomenon, most scientists will list the potential benefits that their results have for society – such as a cure, or a new development in technology. For Morgan, however, the decisive impulse that distinguishes a scientist is his curiosity:

> I said that curiosity was a dangerous quality. It is dangerous not only because of incidental effects like the atomic bomb but also because it is really nothing more or less than a desire for truth. […] The search for truth is, and always has been, a subversive activity. And scholars have learned that they cannot engage in it without an occasional fight. […] They are wary of committing themselves to institutions or beliefs that might impose limitations on them or deliver ready-made answers to their questions.[3]

Science and literature share the subversive potential of curiosity. Both cross borders and carry both danger and renewal. The French author Jules Verne, in his literary creation, conquered the moon 100 years before Neil Armstrong. Mary

---

[3]    Edmund S. Morgan, "What Every Yale Freshman Should Know". *Saturday Review*, XLIII.4 (1960): 13-4, 13.

Wollstonecraft demanded equal educational opportunities for men and women 90 years before compulsory education was introduced in England. As early as in 1818, her daughter Mary Shelley warned the readers of her novel *Frankenstein* about the consequences of a science detached from ethical questions, when the existence of the genetic code was not yet known. Personal curiosity is a driving force of the mind that should not be underestimated; it teaches the curious not to regard everything as true only because it has been printed, and not to blindly accept every statement that sounds convincing without reflection.

Maybe your proseminar paper will not change the world right away. It can, however, help you think critically and independently, to look at a puzzle from different perspectives, and to go beyond your own limits – qualities you are going to need in any career you choose. This book will hopefully guide you on your way.

What this book is not: 1) A systematic introduction to literary and cultural studies comprising descriptions of literary periods, history, and theory. The aim of this book is to help you acquire academic skills and to familiarize you with tools and techniques you are going to need. 2) A word processing course. Although you will receive some tips on how to format your documents, you will not find page-long explanations on how to set a margin or tab stop in Word.

The focus of examples in this book is English and American Studies, yet students of other subject areas in the humanities may encounter similar tasks and difficulties.[4] The convention used are those of literary and cultural studies (deviating regulations for papers in linguistics are stated separately).

For all subjects, however, there is an important principle when writing scientific papers: approach your topic with suf-

---

[4]    The examples in this book are taken from my own work unless otherwise stated. The errors discussed are fictitious, which are, however, based on difficulties characteristic of coursework submitted by students.

ficient sincerity to work carefully, and with a certain playful curiosity to keep asking: What is next?

Throughout this project, I have received a great deal of support and assistance. I would like to offer my special thanks to Dr Nadine Albert. Without the encouragement and professional advice she provided, this book would not exist.

Furthermore, I would like to thank my parents for lending their emotional support and keeping me grounded.

Finally, my grateful thanks are extended to my general dogsbody, Hartmut Hering. His creativity, his eye for detail, and his willingness to give his time so generously have been very much appreciated.

# Chapter 1: Down the Rabbit Hole: Managing Your Studies

> Suddenly a White Rabbit with pink eyes ran close by her. There was nothing so very remarkable in that; nor did Alice think it so very much out of the way to hear the Rabbit say to itself: "Oh dear! Oh dear! I shall be too late!" [...] but, when the Rabbit actually took a watch out of its waistcoat pocket, and looked at it, and then hurried on, Alice started to her feet [...] and burning with curiosity, she ran across the field after it, and was just in time to see it pop down a large rabbit-hole under the hedge. In another moment, down went Alice after it, and never once considered how in the world she was to get out again.[1]

This is how Lewis Carroll's heroine Alice starts her journey to Wonderland. The White Rabbit who is always late in spite of the big watch has been read as a stand-in for the busy, progress-oriented adults of the Victorian world. In your first semesters, you are likely to feel a bit like a cross between the White Rabbit – always running late, no matter how well you think you have organized your time – and Alice – 'burning with curiosity', but at the same time cast into a strange world beyond your comprehension.

Your courses, deadlines for presentations, papers, and exams, meetings of study groups and extracurricular activities, appointments and office hours with university staff, student jobs, opening hours of the library, submitting grant applications, scheduling internships and language courses, setting aside enough time for private study and writing – all this can be quite overwhelming, and, unlike your teachers in school, no one is going to set up a sensible timetable for you. With a bit of strategy, the correct priorities, and some basic time management techniques, however, you can reduce the pressure. If your university has an orientation programme for

---

[1]    Lewis Carroll, *Alice in Wonderland*. Ed. Donald J. Gray. A Norton Critical Edition (New York: Norton, [2]1992), 7-8.

beginning students, do sign up for it. Such programmes include valuable advice on time management and academic reading and writing skills. The same goes for guided tours of your local library or introductory workshops to the library catalogue and databases, which are offered by most libraries at the beginning of the semester. Some libraries have online tutorials about different research topics. Check with your librarian or your library website. You might also consider taking a word processing course for university students. Most tutorials you can find online are about typical office tasks, such as writing letters, formatting a CV, or designing flyers. Make sure you take a specialized class for academic purposes. They are offered cheaply at your local data processing centre.

Not enough time to take even more classes and guided tours? Think of time as an investment; spend it well, on an activity that will save you time later. Knowing how your library is organized will speed up your research and improve the quality of your findings. Knowing your word processing programme well can facilitate your writing. In a class, you will learn about functions you never knew existed, such as generating and updating a table of contents automatically, customizing your style sheets, using spelling and grammar checkers for different languages, or creating a bibliography with plugins. You only create a style sheet once, but you may use it for any paper you have to submit during your studies.

When setting up your schedule for the semester, make sure you have read all module descriptions and exam regulations for your subject. To set up a sensible timetable, it is essential to know which modules have to be completed within a certain time frame (such as language courses or introductory courses) and what the formal requirements and prerequisites are for attending a course – for example, it may be a formal requirement to complete an introductory module in literature to attend an advanced seminar. If there are deadlines for course registration, mark them in your calendar and set an alarm on your phone. Remember to sign up as soon as possible for popular and obligatory modules to avoid disappointment. Be aware that you may not get a place in every course you would like to attend right away, so it is always a good idea to have a backup plan. When you set up a schedule for the semester, also think about how long it will take you to get from A to B, especially if your university is not a campus university. If you can, do not schedule two especially demanding courses after one another. Depending on the organization of your university's exam schedules, this might mean you will also have to take two difficult exams on the same day without a break.

Consider that you need to calculate more time for each course than the hours you spend at university. You require time for reading the primary texts and other materials your course convenor may suggest, for handing in coursework, preparing for presentations, and revising what you have learnt so far. Module handbooks will give you an idea about the average time required to complete the course. Note that university courses proceed faster than you are accustomed to when you leave school, and more time should be assigned to self-study. A rule of thumb: an hour spent at university is an hour spent at home preparing and revising (not including reading of primary texts). If you spend 20 hours a week attending lectures and seminars, your working week will comprise 40 hours. Remember to mark important deadlines and appointments in your calendar. You can use different colours for different types of events (distinguishing, for example, deadlines concerning your studies from doctor's appointments or family birthdays).

When planning your semester, you do not normally think about exams and papers yet. You should, however, aim for a mixture of courses with different forms of assessment, written, oral, portfolio (if available), and research paper. Writing three research papers within the same semester is not the best idea for several reasons: firstly, you will probably have other exams and coursework to hand in during the semester. Even if you start looking for suitable secondary sources and plan your paper early, it is highly unlikely you will start writing before the holidays start. You will have to write and format three complete papers in a matter of four weeks. Supposing each paper is twelve pages of text (excluding title page, table of contents, and list of works cited), you will have to produce nine pages of text per week. For a novice writer, that is at least very difficult to accomplish. Anything unexpected, such as having to re-sit one of your exams, will mess up your schedule. Secondly, writing three papers in the same semester implies that you have the same level of knowledge of research academic writing. You are likely to make the same mistakes in all three papers. If you write one research paper after another, you will benefit from the comments and feedback on the first one when you write the second and third.

One of the most popular methods of time management in consulting books is the Eisenhower matrix. There is no evidence that former US President Dwight D. Eisenhower actually invented or applied this method, but the christening of this principle probably goes back to a speech Eisenhower made during a campus visit to North-Western University, Illinois. Eisenhower quoted from a 'former college president' who had said, "I have two kinds of problems, the urgent and the important. The urgent are not important, and the important are never urgent".[2] The idea behind the Eisenhower matrix is to divide your tasks into four groups:

---

[2]    Dwight D. Eisenhower,"Address at the Second Assembly of the World Council of Churches, Evanston, Illinois, August 19, 1954". *The American Presidency Project*. Web. 1 September 2019.
<https://www.presidency.ucsb.edu/documents/address-the-second-assembly-the-world-council-churches-evanston-illinois>.

| | urgent | |
|---|---|---|
| important | A | B |
| | C | D |

A: urgent, important
B: not urgent, important
C: urgent, not important
D: not urgent, not important

The success of the method, of course, depends on your definitions of 'urgent' and 'important'. You cannot generalize this for everyone in every situation, however, broadly speaking, a task is 'urgent' when it needs your immediate attention; there will be consequences if you put it off. A task is 'important' when it serves your long-term goals, such as completing your studies, having good relations with your family and friends, being healthy and active in your life.[3]

Planning and writing your term paper is a typical B-type of task. Technically, you have known that you are going to write a term paper for this course since you signed up for it. The deadline is not until a few weeks after the end of the semester. Unfortunately, there are other tasks of the A variety that seem more urgent – in-class reading, coursework you have to submit during the semester, filling in the forms for your grant, studying for end-of-semester tests. What we perceive as urgent is always influenced by our immediate concerns. Most people would consider healthy eating and regular exercise as important goals, but with a big exam ahead of them tomorrow, they may still pour over books instead of going to the gym and order a pizza because the exam is more urgent than their lifestyle at this particular point in time. At a different point

---

[3]    The Eisenhower matrix is so widely used that its origins could not be determined. It was popularized by Stephen R. Covey in *The Seven Habits of Highly Effective People* (New York: Free Press, 2004). I would like to thank Lukas Bischof for bringing this method to my attention.

in time, our priorities may change. If you weigh 600 pounds, a healthier lifestyle suddenly rises from priority B to A.

That is why the research paper does not enter your mind until it has become an A-task: the deadline is fast approaching. The only way to avoid the stress and trouble created by putting off B-tasks is to schedule time for them (*e.g.* one hour assigned to writing every day, first thing in the morning) and to make your own deadlines (*e.g.* scheduling a date when you will show your table of contents to your course convenor during his or her office hour).

## Exercises

### Exercise 1.1: Eisenhower Matrix
It is Friday, October 29th. Your semester runs from October 15th to February 8th. Complete the Eisenhower Matrix to achieve the goals from the to-do list below. Can you identify any problems?

### Exercise 1.2: Setting Priorities
Are there any tasks you have categorized as D? What would you do about them?

### Exercise 1.3: Time Management
When would you schedule the dentist's appointment, the guided tour of the library, and the word processing class?

### TO DO list:

- read newsletters and new messages on social networks
- do the dishes in shared kitchen
- dentist's appointment
- buy decorations, drinks and food, choose music for your Halloween party

- term paper in cultural studies (deadline: 15 March)
- read Virginia Woolf, *To the Lighthouse* for literature class on 17 November
- take guided tour of library (every first Monday of a month during the semester, duration: 3 hours)
- pass language test (10 November)
- submit written coursework, translation class (deadline: 8 November)
- pass end-of-term tests, second week of February
- take word processing class, all-day event, available dates: Wed 10 November, Sat 15 January, Wed 9 February, Tue 1 March
- Yoga workshop: 6-7 November
- redecorate kitchen
- give presentation in literature (9 November)

|  | urgent |  |
|---|---|---|
| important | A | B |
|  | C | D |

Every journey begins with the first step – in our case, that is finding a topic you want to write about. Possibly, you will be asked to choose from a list of topics by the course convenor, but perhaps you will have to work out your own proposal from the subject area of the seminar.

In any case, you should make an early effort (not four weeks before the official deadline) to find a topic that makes you curious enough to work on it intensely. If you were bored out of your skull during the *Hamlet* sessions (no pun intended) in your Shakespeare seminar, it makes little sense to write a term paper on the topic of philosophical speeches in *Hamlet*. You are very likely to produce an uninspired paper with insignificant results, or to abandon your project altogether, so why not go for a topic that really interests you in the first place?

Maybe you had rather try one of the comedies, or you can find a more exciting aspect of *Hamlet*, such as the ghostly phenomena or the motif of madness.

Comparative work is also a good way to increase your motivation to do a job. You are not really interested in Renaissance literature? You attended the Shakespeare seminar simply because the course on contemporary literature did not fit into your timetable? Suggest a comparative topic, such as Shakespeare's *Othello* and Blake Morrison's *Othello*-based novel *The Last Weekend*: Othello/Ollie as a rich lawyer, his college friend Iago/Ian as a devious primary school teacher involved in a child abuse scandal, and a Kleenex tissue with suspicious stains found by jealous Ollie in the bathroom of the country house where two couples are spending the weekend. Sounds better?

Topics comparing two texts from different literary periods should nevertheless be treated with caution. Though it can be very exciting and motivating to work out differences, you must not limit yourself to enumerating these differences: "The status of Iago is x, the status of Ian is y, end of story". A comparative presentation of two texts will deal with the forms and functions of intertextuality. How is a Shakespearean motif changed by Morrison, what effect does this have? Which cultural contexts (such as the role of women, combatting racism) have changed, and how does this change affect the classic Shakespearean material? What sources can you use in your body of theory to work with the relations between the two texts (such as Bakhtin's concept of dialogism or Kristeva's intertextuality)?

## 2.1 Phrasing Your Topic

Make sure you have a good title when formulating the topic. Pre-fabricated topics are usually narrow enough to give you a general idea of the work to be written, and broad enough to allow you to set your own priorities. You can still narrow down the scope in the introduction to your paper. Avoid subjective opinions and judgments, or call them into question. Example: The title "The Original Sin: Religious Writers and the Rejection of Curiosity" suggests that curiosity is the original sin and that all religious writers reject it. Do you really know for sure that all religious writers who have ever existed would agree? Avoid such a generalization in the title; it is better to have an open topic that allows a dialectic discussion (pros and cons): "The Original Sin? Religious Writers and the Controversy of Curiosity".

When choosing a topic, make sure that your work reflects the current state of research. This is inevitable if only because of the relatively short text of a term paper. The Freud student Marie Bonaparte published an essay in 1949, claiming that the heartbeat of the murder victim under the floorboards in E.A. Poe's short story "The Tell-Tale Heart" was a direct consequence of Poe's biography; as a toddler in his mother's (an actress's) bedroom, he had become an involuntary witness to her sexual conquests.[1] Such a line of argument based on psychoanalytical and biographical assumptions is no longer considered state of the art in literary studies today.

A provocative, concise or otherwise striking quote may be included in the title, but make sure it "does something for your subject"; just quoting to document your own erudition will be of little use to convince your readers. Another example: "'To Be or Not to Be' – A Characterization of the Protagonist in Shakespeare's *Hamlet*". The quote seems out of place because a connection between the quote and certain traits of the main character is not immediately apparent. Contrast it with this example: "An 'Honourable Murderer'? A Characterization of the Protagonist in Shakespeare's *Othello*". This topic is obviously better than the previous one because Othello himself makes the statement that he wants to be remembered as an "honourable murderer". The title illustrates, also by adding a question mark that does not belong to the original quote, that the paper will examine and critically reflect Othello's self-image.

Once you have decided on a topic, you are not allowed to change the topic on your own. If there are difficulties, contact your advisor. Papers on topics that have not been approved previously will not normally be accepted at universities. Any change of topic (even if it is only a word or translation of a technical term) requires prior agreement.

## 2.2 Topic Development

Once your topic has been formulated, you begin to sound out its limits and ask yourself what solutions and strategies the

---

[1]     Marie Bonaparte, "The Tell-Tale Heart," *The Life and Works of Edgar Allan Poe: A Psycho-Analytic Interpretation* (Albury, Oxfordshire *e.a.*: Imago, 1949), 491-504.

topic requires. Otto Kruse calls this step "topic specification" and suggests the following approach:

1. What is the subject of my term paper? "Subject" can be *e.g.* a material object, a theory, a text or a problem.
2. With which question do I approach the object? Should I present, problematise, explore or analyse a fact?
3. Which material (scientific texts or sources) should be the basis for the writing process?[2]

One of the best-known techniques for developing topics is the collection of materials with the help of brainstorming. Its aim is to try and collect a relatively large amount of topic-related ideas in a very short time.

Example: Brainstorming on "Romantic Elements in Ann Radcliffe's *The Mysteries of Udolpho*"

- Romantic: candlelight, red roses, *kitsch*
- against the Enlightenment
- emotion, irrational, transfigured nature, genius, artist (Valancourt as musician)
- French Revolution
- Poetry, Lake Poets, Graveyard School
- Gothic novel, horror, uncanny
- Nature, description of landscape, Burke: sublime and beautiful
- gloomy castle in Italy, Catholicism, superstition, the supernatural, betrayal of relatives (Emily's aunt)
- characters: Gothic villain (Montoni), damsel in distress (Emily), hero (Valancourt)
- Absent father: St Aubert (unexpected death)
- Secondary sources: first info: lexicon of literature, glossaries, literary history

---

[2]   Otto Kruse, *Keine Angst vor dem leeren Blatt. Ohne Schreibblockaden durchs Studium. Campus Concret* Band 16 (Frankfurt/M: Campus, [10]2004), 87.

In a second step, you can make a substantial classification:

- Clarification of terms romance, Romanticism, definitions
- Opposition to the Enlightenment and its concept of reason, emotion, irrational, transfigured nature, concept of genius (role of the artist? Artist in *Udolpho*: musician Valancourt)
- Political influences: French Revolution
- What subtopics?
  - Poems at the beginning of chapters of *Udolpho*, poetry, Lake Poets, Graveyard School (influence on poems in *Udolpho*?)
  - Genre classification of *Udolpho*: Gothic, horror *vs.* terror, Radcliffe's own theory, supernatural explained
  - Setting: Description of nature, Burke: the sublime; gloomy castle in Italy (Catholicism, superstition, needs Enlightenment)
  - Plot – damsel in distress pursued by a villain, betrayal (aunt)
  - Characters – Villain (Montoni), damsel in distress (Emily), hero (Valancourt), absent father: St Aubert (unexpected death)
  - What kind of secondary literature? Robert Miles on Radcliffe, Edmund Burke on the sublime and beautiful, M.H. Abrams, Mirror and Lamp, Sigmund Freud, "The Uncanny"

*Clustering*[3] is a possibility to visualize brainstorming developed by the German-American Gabriele L. Rico. In a cluster, the central term/theme is placed in the middle. Then you collect associations, which are grouped around it.[4] Each term

---

[3]  Gabriele L. Rico, "What is Clustering?". *Writing the Natural Way*. Web. 22 March 2013. <http://www.gabrielerico.com/home/index.php?option=com_content&task=view&id=14&Itemid=69>.

[4]  More useful hints on working with brainstorming and clustering: Franziska Egle, *teachSam – Lehren und Lernen online*. Web. 20 September 2019. <http://www.teachsam.de/arb/krea/krea_clust_0.htm>.

within the cluster can in turn create its own cluster: "A cluster is like an expanding universe, and each word is a potential galaxy: each galaxy in turn may throw out its own universe".[5]

## 2.3 Alternative Methods of Topic Development

If you have already written a number of term papers, you have probably run into the limits of brainstorming and clustering. Sometimes, looking at the empty sheet or screen in front of you, ideas just will not come. In such a case, you might want to try an altogether different method.

### Finding a topic: The imaginary bookshelf

The imaginary bookshelf originates in creative writing. It may not be your cup of tea if you are not a visual person, but if you have reached an impasse, it may help you get back on track with your writing. I first came across this exercise in a creative writing workshop with Adam Thorpe in Berlin in 2006, when I was working on my PhD thesis. I have adapted it slightly to fit academic writing. It is a mixture between an association game and a visualisation exercise. You may want to try this with a partner, taking turns so you can watch out for each other when moving around with your eyes closed, and take notes of what your partner is saying. If you prefer to try this alone, do not move around physically, and record your voice during the exercise so you remember all details later.

Imagine yourself at a scholarly library – not your own university library, unless it is a special one that sparks your imagination. You may want to think of an old-fashioned, antique

---

5    Rico, "What is Clustering?", n.pag.

library such as the Bodleian library in Oxford, one of the old-
est libraries in Europe, dating back to the fourteenth century;
or you may feel more at home in an avantgarde design library,
such as the Qatar National Library or the futuristic library of
Tianjin in China.[6] What matters is that you feel comfortable
in your surroundings (even the forbidden books section at the
Hogwarts library may do). Close your eyes and envision yourself at that library. Behind you, there is a shelf with hundreds
of books on your subject area. Get up from your chair and
walk to the shelf (physically, if there is enough space). Take
one of the books from the shelf (raise your hand, pull it from
the shelf). Describe what it looks like. Is it hardcover, paper-
back, or simply a bound manuscript archived for later reference? Is it old or new? Is it a heavy tome or a thin volume?
How does the paper feel? Does it smell? Now look at the
cover. Read the author's name – it is blurry at first, but when
you look more closely, you can see it is your name in print.
Can you read the title? That is the topic of your paper.

Now browse the book and open it somewhere in the middle. Start reading. What is the page number? What is the first
word on the page? The second word? And so on. The secret
is not to make up the words, but to read them in the imaginary
book. When you cannot read it and the lines are blurry, move
the book further away or closer to your eyes until it becomes
clear.

---

6   For a slide show of extraordinary libraries around the world, *cf.* Andrea
    Lo,"How Beautiful Design Is Keeping Libraries Relevant in the Digital Era".
    *CNN Style*. Web. 23 April 2018. <https://edition.cnn.com/style/article/mod-
    ern-libraries/index.html>.

## Developing a Topic: Six Thinking Hats (Edward de Bono)

The Six Thinking Hats method was developed by Maltese physician, psychologist and consultant Edward de Bono.[7] It was developed for groups, but you can use it to look at your subject from different perspectives. Again, I have adapted the method for developing a topic in literary studies. Other than the bookshelf method, the thinking hats will not help you find a topic, but the purpose is to critically reflect a topic you are about to choose or have already chosen. The idea is to mentally put on a coloured hat and take the position associated with that colour. Set a timer for each colour and take notes. The colours are:

- White for analytical thinking: data, facts, figures. When was the text written? By whom? What is the genre of the text? What characteristics of genre and literary period are associated with such texts? What are important words in the title of your paper, how are they defined in a glossary, dictionary, …?
- Red for emotional thinking: how do you feel about the text and your topic question? Is it interesting or boring to you? Are you afraid of the level of difficulty, or embracing a challenge? In short: everything that should not go into your paper, but your intuition may still point you towards discontinuities and problems in the text or topic, or your general attitude.
- Black for pessimism: what can possibly go wrong in your analysis or the writing process? What are the risks of writing such a paper as you are planning? Do not make up an alien invasion that will stop you from writing. You are looking for real arguments here, just from a pessimistic perspective.

---

[7]    Edward de Bono, *Six Thinking Hats. An Essential Approach to Business Management* (Boston: Little Brown, 1985), 207.

- Yellow for optimism: what are the advantages of writing such a paper as you are planning?
- Green for innovation: what new ideas can you add to the project right now? Maybe something about the new theory you have read about, or a different, unconventional way of reading a well-known text? Be creative, collect all ideas that come into your mind, and do not judge. All creative input is welcome.
- Blue for order: this is the hat you wear last. Structure everything you have written down so far. Evaluate, judge your thoughts.

After evaluating your notes, you may want to do another round of thinking hats.

**Exercises**

**Exercise 2.1: Finding a Topic**
In your opinion, are the following topics suitable for an academic paper? If not, can you improve them?

a) Aspects of the Role of Women in the Marriage Concept of the *Regency Period* in Jane Austen's *Pride and Prejudice*
b) Representations and Images of Women in Shakespeare's *Othello* and Blake Morrison's *The Last Weekend*
c) Shakespeare's *Hamlet*: A Psychoanalytical Approach
d) The Role of Evil in Shakespeare's *Macbeth*
e) Blood Imagery in the Third Act of Shakespeare's *Macbeth*
f) Comparative Presentation of Key Elements, Plot Structures and Characters in the Novels *The Mysteries of Udolpho* by Ann Radcliffe and *Zofloya, or the Moor* by Charlotte Dacre as the Basis for *Terror* and *Horror* in the Eighteenth-Century Gothic Novel

g) Functions of the *Gothic* in Jane Austens *Northanger Abbey*
h) The Lack of Persuasiveness of Mary Wollstonecraft's Feminism in *A Vindication of the Rights of Woman*

### Exercise 2.2: Topic Development

Try one of the developing methods on the following topic: Writing a Good Research Paper in English and American Studies

# Chapter 3: Research

When students come to see their supervisor in his or her office hours, they often claim not to have found any secondary literature on their topic, even if it is popular and frequently covered in academic publications. In the following discussion, it turns out that this happens for the following reasons: first of all, many students do not have the necessary skills to make the most of all available sources of information; they have never taken a tour of their university library and are not familiar with the databases available on their subject area. Although most of them have a high affinity with technology, they do not know how to evaluate sources. Secondly, they often have a wrong concept of what exactly secondary literature is.

## 3.1 "Secondary Literature"

By secondary literature, many students understand student guides for a work of literature, in which, for example, the plot is summarized, characters are analyzed, difficult vocabulary is explained, and the most important themes and motifs of the novel are discussed. A student guide such as *Cliff's Notes*, which is widely used in the English-speaking world, is only a part of secondary literature. If this type of secondary literature does not exist for a given text, this does not mean that no other type of secondary literature is available. The secondary literature for a text includes everything that has been written about a particular work: Articles in anthologies, conference proceedings and professional journals, reviews in daily newspapers,[1] philosophical, political or religious works from

---

[1]   Promising sources for reviews of contemporary works are the websites and archives of quality newspapers, for example the *Times Literary Supplement*. For older texts, you might want to search *The English Review*. There are also

the same period, introductions on the genre or period, other works of the same author, similar works of other authors.

A rule of thumb: Read neither too little nor too much. You do not have to read every book from cover to cover. In many cases, only individual chapters are relevant. Do not rely solely on the internet for advice just because you cannot be bothered to take a five-minute walk to the library.

This section introduces you to potential sources of information and their useful and efficient use. At the beginning of a semester or term, university libraries offer free tours and trainings in which you can learn how to use the library, especially the reading room, and the existing databases. They also provide tips on how to search efficiently. Some libraries have also made available their tutorials and self-study materials online, for example on virtual learning platforms.

## 3.2 Library Catalogues

They provide information on what titles are available on site or in a library network. Attention: You will only receive hits available from the libraries listed in the catalogue. For a course presentation or a term paper, a local search in the library catalogue or online public access catalogue (sometimes abbreviated OPAC) of your university should be sufficient in most cases. For a research paper in an advanced seminar, a BA or MA thesis or dissertation, you should also use the interlibrary loan option.

Example: You have to give a presentation on Edmund Burke, *Inquiry into the Origins of our Ideas of the Sublime and Beautiful*. Now you are looking for interpretations, summaries and comments on the original text. Be sure to vary

---

newspaper archives online, which may be free or paywall blocked. Your local library is likely to have subscriptions for historical newspaper archives. Check the "databases" section of your library website for details.

your search terms. Search for titles, authors and keywords, but also for overviews and readers on Romanticism or on the late eighteenth century. Often you will also find individual chapters on works in biographies. Combine search terms differently. Here are a few examples of how you can proceed (you will probably have more ideas):

> Burke + Edmund, Burke + Sublime, Sublime + Beautiful, Sublime + critical + theory, Burke + philosophy, Burke + Romanticism, Romanticism + theory, Burke + aesthetics, Burke + aesthetic + programme, Burke + Edmund + commentary, Burke + sublime + notes, Radcliffe + landscape, Romanticism + literary + theory, Burke + Edmund + biography, …

**HINT:** Also search specifically for biographies. These often contain a list of works cited that can serve as a basis for further research. Use wildcards specifically. Wildcards are characters that can be substituted; for example, with "*romant\**" you can cover the search terms *romantic, Romantics, romantical, Romanticism,* Romantik, Romantiker, romantisch, *romantique, romanticismo*[2] with one search.

The question mark (?, sometimes also the underscore _) stands for exactly one character, the asterisk (*, sometimes the percentage sign %), stands for any number of characters (including zero). Patterns like "romant*", which contain wildcards and stand for whole strings, are called regular expressions in computer science.

## 3.3 Bibliographies and Databases

A bibliography, which can be available in electronic or printed form, provides information on which titles have been written and published on a particular topic. For English and American

---

[2]     To exclude hits in languages you do not understand, customize the search
options of your library catalogue.

Studies, for example, the *MLA International Bibliography* is the first point of contact. The bibliography does not provide any information on availability though.[3] Databases are electronic data collections – the spectrum can range from the bibliography over the *Encyclopaedia Britannica* up to dictionaries.

## Searching for journal articles with bibliographies

By the term 'journal', scholars do not mean *Better Homes and Gardens* or *Cosmopolitan*. In so-called periodicals, the expert journals of a certain field of research, the latest methods and results of research are published, and dialogue within the scientific community is initiated. Journal articles reflect the current state of the art in your discipline.

Your introductory course in literature and the homepage of your university library will provide you with information about the most important journals in English and American Studies in your country. National and international associations for the study of English, such as the *ESSE* (*European Society for the Study of English*), publish their own journals, for example, *The European Messenger*.

Whereas in book publications, years can pass from the initial idea to the finished book, many periodicals appear quarterly. Particularly in the field of contemporary literature, it takes time for the first monographs on new authors to be available from libraries, while in journals you can find hits after a relatively short time.

---

[3]    Bibliographies at the end of an academic term paper or other publication are also referred to as bibliographies. Such bibliographies can of course also be used for further research. This works according to the snowball system: you check the footnotes or the bibliography of a book or article for more works on the same topic.

If you use only books in your term paper, it will be difficult to mirror the current state of research on your topic. You will lose points in your assessment – as you will if you complain to your supervisor that you have not found anything on your topic, and it turns out that you have not consulted the MLA database yet.

- Click "Databases" on the main page of your university library. For example, call up the *MLA International Bibliography*.
- Search for articles on your topic. Again: the search term makes a big difference! Attention: The hits you receive do not yet mean that all these articles are also available at your local library!
- Search the catalogue for journals which are available locally (many databases have a direct link to your local options or a useful follow-up search). You can then order the article via your library catalogue.
- If all else fails, there are also document delivery services (such as SUBITO), from which you can order articles for a reasonable fee.

**Conference Proceedings**

In addition to journal articles, conference proceedings are an important source of information on the current state of research on a specific topic. These are anthologies published by the organizers following an expert conference containing written versions of the papers presented. As book publications come at a considerable cost for editorial boards – the so-called printing cost subsidy –, organizing teams of conferences may also co-operate with a journal and then publish a special issue on the topic of the conference instead.

### 3.4 Local Libraries

If your department has its own branch library, *i.e.* a library that is part of your university library system, but contains specialized books for a particular subject, you can go directly to the shelf and browse through individual titles. Familiarize yourself with the systematics of the library as soon as possible. There are many different ways of organizing a library, such as primary literature followed by secondary literature, date of birth of the author. Similar books are often grouped together in sections. If you attend a tutorial, ask your tutor to give you a guided tour of your branch library.

Not all libraries allow you to view every book before you borrow it. Especially in big university libraries, there is a reading room, but with the exception of reference works the books have to be pre-ordered via internet/intranet.

If there is a possibility to have direct access to the bookshelves, remember to always browse through the overviews of the genre and the literary period – if your paper is about Ann Radcliffe's *The Mysteries of Udolpho*, do not just look for Ann Radcliffe, but also consult general works on Romanticism and on the Gothic novel. With some luck they will contain chapters that refer directly to Ann Radcliffe and *The Mysteries of Udolpho*.

Reference works are not detailed enough to be the only sources for papers. In many cases, however, they are useful as prompts for further research. Examples of such reference works are:

- *ODNB (Oxford Dictionary of National Biography)*
- *Oxford Companion to English Literature*
- *Cambridge Guide to Literature in English*
- *Encyclopaedia Britannica*
- *Oxford Dictionary of Art*

## 3.5 Using Search Engines and Websites in Academia

Often an internet search is your first impulse to learn something new about a topic – anyone who carelessly asks a question on the internet whose answer he could have found himself with the help of a search engine will receive "GIYF" ("Google is your friend") in reply. Of course, Google also remains your friend while you are doing research.

With your academic work, you can expand your circle of friends to specialized search engines like CiteSeer[X], Scirus, BASE, CORE, MS Academic, and Google Scholar. As with Google, the order of your search results is determined by how often a particular article is accessed, but unlike Google, Google Scholar also takes into account where the article was published, how current the article is, and how often it was quoted in academic literature, a piece of information that scientists can find in the „Hirsch-Index".[4] For queries on search engines, the same advice applies as for searching in databases:

* **Vary the search terms** . Do not search for title and author exclusively, but also for bibliographies and biographies (they often contain references to useful secondary literature and link collections).
* **Use short, concise *strings*** (strings of words enclosed in quotation marks) and the "Advanced Search" option.

If you want to quote an internet source in your paper, finding a website which provides information does not suffice. It must also meet the criteria of scientific excellence. In its "White

---

[4]   In theory, that means: the more often a publication is quoted, the more influential it is in its field. In practice, however, one cannot automatically deduce success or performance from the frequency of citation, since the Hirsch index can be changed or manipulated by various factors (*e.g.* field of science, multiple authors, self-quotations, networking, name changes) and erroneous publications can also result in a large number of citations (namely to criticize the errors). In the humanities, the Hirsch index is not as common as in the natural sciences.

Paper Safeguarding Good Scientific Practice", the *Deutsche Forschungsgemeinschaft* (German Research Foundation) defines the following criteria for scientific excellence:

- observing professional standards,
- documenting results,
- consistently questioning one's own findings,
- practising strict honesty with regard to the contributions of partners, competitors and predecessors.[5]

A citable internet source must document and constantly review both its approach and its own sources as well as its results, and include the current state of research. So-called study guides such as *Sparknotes*, on which you will find a summary of Shakespeare's *Macbeth*, does not normally provide any references and bibliographies, but your free annual horoscope and the latest flirt tips. What you find on such websites is a number of very general summaries of the main topics and motifs of a text, all of them without academic evidence and too superficial to be used in an academic term paper. Often these texts are identical on several portals, without the copyright being clarified; consequently, errors reproduce themselves. Needless to say that you cannot quote from these sites in an academic paper.

The same applies to private websites. Around some authors, for example Jane Austen, an online cult has been established, which has generated huge data collections with all imaginable information about her novels, for example the *Republic of Pemberley*.[6] Since such sites are usually run by fans and their interest in Jane Austen has no scientific objec-

---

[5]    Deutsche Forschungsgemeinschaft, "White Paper Safeguarding Good Scientific Practice". (Weinheim: WILEY-VCH, 1998). Web. 14 August 2019. <https://www.dfg.de/download/pdf/dfg_im_profil/reden_stellungnahmen/download/empfehlung_wiss_praxis_1310.pdf>.

[6]    *Republic of Pemberley*. Webmaster: Myretta Robens. 2004. Web. 14 August 2019. <http://www.pemberley.com/>.

tive, but consists in social networking of like-minded people, such sites are not suitable sources for a research paper either (unless you conduct a case study on the fan cult around Jane Austen for your Cultural Studies module).

Student essays and term papers are also unhelpful as sources. As a student, you know from your own experience that you have to try your hand at academic writing in your first term papers. The quality of your work will increase with experience. The same goes for other students; student papers that have been published on a private website or in online collections should only be read with a very critical eye, if at all, and not quoted.

BA and MA theses are on the threshold between programmes of study and academic qualification. As a rule, they meet standards more adequately than student theses and can be used under certain circumstances: if, for example, the subject matter is so topical that no monographs are available. You would not exactly use a thesis as a source if your paper is on a popular topic like Shakespeare's *Hamlet* or Milton's *Paradise Lost*, with lots of high-quality publications available. If you are doing research on young contemporary authors such as Helen Walsh or Jen Hadfield, studies on their works are scarce. If you have identified only a handful of publications on your topic, there is nothing wrong with consulting an MA thesis you have found on the internet, as long as you read it critically.

Popular, but still unsuitable as an academic source: the online encyclopaedia, the most prominent example being *Wikipedia*. It can be edited by anyone at any time, regardless of the qualification of its author and without a formalized review process by experts in the field of study. That is why online encyclopaedias may not be quoted in a research paper.[7] This is not as great a loss as one might assume at first

---

[7]    The exception to the rule is papers concerned with online culture, in which the encyclopaedia is not the secondary source, but the object of study.

glance. If you take the trouble to read footnotes and biblio-graphical references in *Wikipedia* articles, you will soon realize that the same (and more) pieces of information can be lo-cated in reliable academic sources from your trusted library with relatively little effort.

## 3.6 Checklist: Academic Internet Sources...

- provide all necessary information for an entry in MLA for-mat[8] (author, organization, last update)
- are subject to a certain degree of "quality control", *i.e.* they cannot be edited by anyyone at any time
- **give evidence** on the basis of other academic sources
- **clearly separate** the author's own thoughts from those of others
- are characterized by **a neutral, scientific (usually not journalistic) writing style**
- do not reproduce the personal opinion of the author (ex-ception: book or film reviews[9]), but express a well-founded academic point of view
- specify a contact who is legally responsible for the content of the site
- (mostly) have a more sober, factual layout, unlike *e.g.* "fansites" or private websites (uniform color scheme, no playful fonts, no gimmicks, pictures as real illustrations, rarely as decoration)

---

[8]    The Modern Language Association has defined the so-called MLA style as a universal formatting standard for academic work in the humanities. Chicago Style, for example, offers an alternative to the MLA style. Please contact your department to find out which style is preferable.

[9]    Only reviews in newspapers (arts pages of the so-called quality papers) and journals are suitable for scientific works, no reviews in personal blogs or cus-tomer reviews in online bookstores.

Examples for reliable internet sources which can be cited in research papers:

- the online versions of dissertations and postdoctoral theses, online journals or online editions of academic journals, such as *American Literature*, which contains articles on all periods of American literature as well as detailed reviews: <http://americanliterature.dukejournals.org/>
- the pages of professional associations (such as the European Society for the Study of English (<https://essenglish.org>)
- Pages of museums, libraries, or governmental institutions
- Websites of universities or state-funded research projects (*e.g.* Research Training Groups)
- official homepage of a contemporary author
- Websites of English-language daily newspapers and their archives (*e.g.* for reviews), list of all newspapers in the United Kingdom which can be accessed online: <http://www.wrx.zen.co.uk/britnews.htm>, international: <http://www.onlinenewspapers.com/>, historical American newspapers at the Library of Congress: <http://chroniclingamerica.loc.gov/about/>

All sources used in the main text of your work must be listed with a complete record in your bibliography. **It is not sufficient to indicate the URL (web address).**

A bibliographic record of an article on a website in MLA style consists of the author's name, the title of the article in quotation marks, the name of the website or organization in italics, the date you accessed the website, and the internet address (URL). For differences between MLA7 and MLA8, see Chapter 9, this volume. Example:

MLA7:

Frigg, Roman and Stephan Hartmann. "Models in Science". *The Stanford Encyclopedia of Philosophy* (Fall 2012 edi-

tion). Web. 20 May 2018. <http://plato.stanford.edu/archives/fall2012/entries/models-science/>.
MLA 8 :
Frigg, Roman *e.a.* "Models in Science". *The Stanford Encyclopedia of Philosophy*, 20 May 2018, http://plato.stanford.edu/archives/fall2012/entries/models-science/.

The following abbreviations apply: *n.p. (no publisher given)*, *n.d. (no date of publication given)*, *n.pag. (no pagination)*.

## 3.7 Are Online Sources 'Less Acceptable' Than Others?

Although the use of the internet has become an integral part of academia, there is a persistent rumour among students that an internet page is not a correct source, is marked as "wrong" anyway, or must always be additionally documented by a print medium.

That is not the case, provided that you have checked your source for accuracy and have substantiated your quote or paraphrase accordingly. There is no reason why an academic article in a journal published exclusively online should be less 'valuable' than the same article in the print edition. To arrive at a differentiated view of your topic, aim at a mixture of different media. At most half of your sources should be from the internet.

- Always refer to several **different sources**, especially when presenting the current state of research. Otherwise the impression may arise that you have obtained all your wisdom from a single website.
- **Combine** internet sources and literature from your library research. Compare and contrast sources with each other.

- Use **primary texts** from the internet only if absolutely necessary (*e.g.* if they are out of print and cannot be obtained via interlibrary loan).
  Widespread digital text collections are, for example, *Project Gutenberg*, the San Francisco non-profit digital library *Internet Archive*, *Questia Online Library*, or *eBooks@Adelaide* based at the University of Adelaide.

To provide a reliable basis for academic work, there are critical editions of primary texts. A critical edition attempts to remove obvious errors and to present the text in a form that considers editorial processes and different varieties of the same text. Therefore, a printed edition from an established series (Norton Critical Edition, Oxford World's Classics, for Shakespeare: Arden Edition) is always preferable to a digital text collection which may be based on any edition available to the volunteers. As critical editions tend to be more expensive than student editions, you can work with your student edition in class and borrow the critical edition from the library for your paper.

**Dissertations** can be used as scientific sources, but even in this case you should be critical of the texts. To obtain a doctorate, in many countries the thesis has to be published, no matter if the candidate is planning to pursue an academic career. Pay attention to writing style, register and argumentation structure. Is the argument convincing? Are style and register appropriate for an academic paper? In the case of older works, look for later publications by the same author. The lack of reviews of a dissertation is not normally a good way to assess the quality of a work. Since many dissertations are published every year, an author's 'first book' is seldom reviewed at all.

## 3.8 What You Know – What You Should Know

This chapter describes a selection of reference books and the types of information they contain. You can find a detailed list of titles in the appendix to this volume.

### Literary History, Anthologies

If you have attended a seminar on a literary period of which you have little previous knowledge, or if you would like to familiarize yourself with the historical context of a text for your thesis, it makes sense to take a closer look at a work of literary history. In the course of your studies, you should work through at least one complete book of literary history. Compare different works with each other and choose the compilation that suits you best. Note that literary studies tends to borrow terminology from other disciplines, such as architecture (Gothic novel), art (Renaissance), linguistics (Old English literature), or politics (Restoration). Therefore, the division into literary periods may differ between the works.

### Encyclopaedias of Authors, Biographies, Quotations

If you are looking for information about the biography and works of a writer, you will find reliable information in an encyclopaedia of authors or in the *ODNB* (*Oxford Dictionary of National Biography*). The *ODNB* contains biographies from other fields than literature, such as monarchs, politicians, artists, scientists, and philosophers.

You have come across a quotation, but cannot remember who said it, or you are looking for a fitting quote for your introduction? The *Oxford Dictionary of Quotations* contains over 20,000 quotes.

## Glossaries, Terminology, Handbooks

You have read a technical term and do not know exactly what it means? You want to know something about Cultural Materialism without having to read an entire textbook? Consult a glossary, a dictionary of terminology, or a specialist dictionary. Historical overviews of intellectual history, literary and cultural movements, philosophical schools and their most important representatives are provided by handbooks of literary and cultural theory.

A dictionary of philosophy contains definitions and information about the origins and developments of philosophical terms, their changes of meaning as well as the biographies of influential philosophers.

## Literary Theory

Literary theory is indispensable for the analysis of texts. Anyone who reads secondary literature on a particular primary text should be able to understand the underlying methods and theoretical considerations. A follower of Freudian psychoanalysis will read Henry James' *The Turn of the Screw* from a completely different point of view from that of a feminist scholar. A critic indebted to New Historicism will not interpret a literary text at all until he has consulted non-literary sources from the same period and considered marginalized groups of society. A poststructuralist will even doubt the stability of the text itself. Therefore, you should get an overview of various theoretical approaches as early as possible in your studies.

Introductions to literary theory can be regarded as a kind of "travel guide". As with literary history, each of these works has its strengths and weaknesses; you should look at several of them and choose a book which fits your method of study.

**Theoretical "Standard Works"**

It would be an almost infinite undertaking to list all common literary theorems that students of English and American studies should have read during their studies. Nevertheless, there are a few theoretical works that you will encounter time and time again during your studies and to which numerous discussions will be linked in your seminars. For example, Ian Watt's *The Rise of the Novel* is a must for anyone interested in Romantic theory. On the effect and function of storytelling, read Wolfgang Iser (*The Act of Reading*) , Franz Stanzel (*The Theory of Narrative*) and Gérard Genette (*Narrative Discourse*). If you are interested in postcolonial literature, Homi Bhaba or Edward Said come into play.

You will find detailed reading lists and orientation aids in courses for exam preparation, in study guides, or on the websites of universities.

**Bibliographies and Databases**

Bibliographies are lists and/or literature databases sorted by year, which provide information on books, journal articles, dissertations and commemorative publications. Never claim that you cannot find any secondary literature until you have checked these. Most bibliographies are available online, whereas the printed versions are slowly dying out. Access to databases can usually be gained via the homepage of your university library. Some databases can only be accessed from the internal network of your university, but not via an external provider. Tip: Ask your university's computer centre about external access to the university's network.

Known bibliographies for English and American Studies are:

- *MLA (= Modern Language Association) International Bibliography of Books and Articles on the Modern Languages and Literatures*.
- *ABELL (= Annual Bibliography of English Language and Literature)*.
- *YWES (= The Year's Work in English Studies)*
- *AES (= Abstracts of English Studies)*
- *AHL (= America: History and Life)*
- *BLLDB (= Bibliography of Linguistic Literature DataBase)*

Whereas a bibliography merely provides information about the existence, but not the availability of a text, there are full-text databases from which you can download complete articles, occasionally also book chapters.

- **JSTOR**
  Interdisciplinary database where you can find scans from previous issues of professional journals.
  <http://www.jstor.org/>
- **PROJECT MUSE**
  Access to full texts from academic journals in the humanities and social sciences.
  <http://muse.jhu.edu/>
- **Questia Online Library**
  A full-text database of over 5000 e-texts whose copyright has expired. You will find both great English classics and rare texts that are no longer available in print.
  <http://www.questia.com/publicdomainindex>
- **Times Literary Supplement Historical Archive (Gale)**
  "The *TLS* Historical Archive contains the full text of all issues of the *Times Literary Supplement* from the first issue in 1902 to 2005 and presents a panorama of the works of important writers and thinkers during this period. It also contains reviews from the fields of theatre, cinema, music

and exhibitions".[10] It is particularly relevant if you are working on a task relating to contemporary literature for which no monographs are available yet. Check the website of your local university library for direct access options. There may also be national licenses available to individuals on registration.

- **Voice of the Shuttle (VoS) – Literature in English**
  Voice of the Shuttle is an extensive humanities database for research and teaching; it contains links to online journals, glossaries, text archives, job offers, online courses, conferences, and much more.
  <http://vos.ucsb.edu/>

## Academic Writing and Style Guides

### MLA Style and Chicago Style
In English and American Studies, two standards are used to format scientific papers: MLA Style and Chicago Style (learn more about styles in Chapters 8 and 9).
For MLA style, see

- Joseph Gibaldi, *MLA Handbook for Writers of Research Papers*, 7th edition (New York: MLA, 2009), henceforth referred to as **"MLA7", OR**
- Joseph Gibaldi, *MLA Handbook*, 8th edition (New York: MLA, 2016), henceforth referred to as **"MLA8".**
- "MLA Formatting and Style Guide". *Purdue Online Writing Lab*. Web. 14 August 2019.

---

[10]    "Times Literary Supplement Historical Archive 1902 – 2005 / TLS ". Trans. SB. Web. 26 September 2019.
<https://www.nationallizenzen.de/angebote/nlproduct.2006-03-10.623677 5959>.

- <https://owl.purdue.edu/owl/research_and_citation/mla_style/mla_formatting_and_style_guide/mla_formatting_and_style_guide.html>.

For Chicago Style, see:
- Turabian, Kate L. *A Manual for Writers of Research Papers, Theses, and Dissertations: Chicago Style for Students and Researchers*. Ed. Wayne C. Booth and Gregory G. Colomb. Chicago: University of Chicago Press, [9]2018.

**Books on Academic Writing**
In 1959, William Strunk and E.B. White published their best-selling book *The Elements of Style*, which *Time* has named one of the 100 most influential books written in English since the 1920s. Ever since, guides on language and style have flooded bookstores – yet the question of what it really means to 'write well' is still controversial. Some titles you may want to have a look at: William Strunk, E.B. White*, The Elements of Style* (General, 2019), William Zinsser, *On Writing Well* (Harper, 2016), Ken Smith, *Junk English* (Blast, 2001), and Bill Walsh, *The Elephants of Style* (McGraw-Hill, 2004), Dirk Siepmann, John D. Gallagher, Mike Hannay, Lachlan Mackenzie, *Writing in English: A Guide for Advanced Learners* (Francke, 2011).

If you are already a little more advanced in your academic work, for example, if you would like to start on your MA thesis or dissertation, the following title is recommended: Joan Bolker, *Writing Your Dissertation in Fifteen Minutes a Day* (Henry and Holt, 1998).

## Exercises

### Exercise 3.1: Identifying Academic Sources

Open a browser and display the following Internet sources. Try to assess whether they are sources that you could quote in your research paper.

a) https://www.theguardian.com/books/2017/jun/11/missing-fay-adam-thorpe-review
b) http://www.angelfire.com/md2/timewarp/burke.html
c) https://janeausten.fandom.com/wiki/The_Jane_Austen_Wiki
d) http://www.victorianweb.org/philosophy/sublime/burke.html
e) https://www.britishmuseum.org/research/publications/online_journals/bmsaes/issue_19/davies_oconnell.aspx
f) http://www.shakespeare-online.com/sources/hamlet sources.html

Note: Due to the fluctuation of Internet sources, not all links may be available any more. At the time of going to press, all information was up to date.

### Exercise 3.2: Reference Works

a) For what purposes would you use the following sources in your academic work

- Online encyclopaedia (*e.g. Wikipedia*)
- conference proceedings
- *ODNB*
- *MLA International Bibliography*

b) Where would you look?
- Freud's model of the psyche was briefly mentioned in the seminar, but you do not know what it is.

- You need a brief description of Freud's model of the psyche for a footnote in your paper.
- You are writing a paper analysing Henry James' *The Turn of the Screw* from a psychological point of view and need a body of theory on Freudian psychoanalysis.

### Exercise 3.3: Library Research

With this exercise you will train your research skills. Photocopy the questionnaire below and try to find the required information only with the help of your local library. For each hit, state the exact location (with author/editor, title, publisher, year, page). It is not important to answer all questions correctly in this exercise; most of these questions can be answered using a search engine on the internet. This exercise is designed to help you find your way around your library, locate scientific sources quickly and efficiently, and lose some of your shyness about the library.

a) What is a zeugma?
   found in (full bibliographical reference):

_____

b) Name a representative of the literary approach of *New Historicism*.
   found in (full bibliographical reference):

_____

c) Find a journal article on the works of Adam Thorpe.
   found in (full bibliographical reference):

_____

d) Which recent publication by Catherine Spooner is concerned with *Dark Shadows*?
   found in (full bibliographical reference):

_____

e) Who was Gerard Manley Hopkins?
   found in (full bibliographical reference):

_____

f) When is the literary period of Romanticism in England?
   Name three Romantic poets in English literature.
   found in (full bibliographical reference):

_____

g) Who wrote this: "'I think it great affectation not to quote
   oneself"?
   found in (full bibliographical reference):

_____

# Chapter 4: Presentation

Why consider a chapter on presentation a part of "academic skills" when you are already familiar with presentations from your school days? As a matter of fact, oral presentations in school tend to help only the student giving the presentation. For everyone else, they are a welcome opportunity to catch up on sleep. There are hundreds of guidebooks, websites, tutorials, and handouts available on presenting, most of which, including my own tentative attempts at giving students advice on their presentations, are limited to commonplaces: "do not cram your slides with tiny writing", "speak loudly and clearly", "take your hands out of your pockets". This is all very well, however, it will not help you become a better presenter. That is why this chapter takes a slightly different approach.

Higher education didactics speaks of three key factors interacting in a teaching-learning triangle, consisting of teacher, students, and topic.[1] In your presentation that is you, your audience, and your material. It is only by a balanced interplay of all three of them that you can leave the sphere of school, where presentations are designed almost exclusively for assessment, and arrive at a scholarly take on presenting material to others, which is to provide a different perspective and prompt others (and yourself) to think critically, evaluate, and increase their knowledge.

---

[1]  Andreas Böss-Ostendorf and Holger Senft, *Einführung in die Hochschullehre. Ein Didaktik-Coach* (Budrich: Opladen and Farmington Hills, MI, 2010), 95-125.

## 4.1 Your Audience: Example, "A Presentation Gone Wrong"

All students in a seminar were asked to give a twenty-minute paper in teams of two. They were asked to submit a one-page handout to the supervisor, Mrs Smith, providing an overview of the structure of the paper. Emily and Isabella were big fans of *Twilight*, so they chose "The Vampire – then and now" as their topic for a course presentation. They did a lot of research, read books and articles on the topic, met weekly to review the material and plan their presentation together. The draft looked good, but with a four-page handout, it was very detailed, so Mrs Smith asked them to shorten their historical overview and reminded them of the time limit.

On the day of their presentation, Emily and Isabella were eager to tell everyone what they had found out. Emily started giving a well-researched presentation with lots of historical facts that were not on her handout. After ten minutes of historical introduction to vampires, Emily was still stuck in the early nineteenth century. The supervisor told her that her time was up, and it was Isabella's turn. Emily was exasperated, as she had not even come to *Dracula*, the best part of her presentation. Isabella said that her part depended on Emily's remarks on *Dracula*, so the supervisor grudgingly gave Emily another three minutes.

Ten minutes later, Isabella finally started on her subtopic. Looking around, Mrs Smith saw only empty and confused faces. During Isabella's talk, there was a considerable amount of noise in the classroom, students whispering to each other, typing on their smartphones, or going through their manuscripts. At the close of the course meeting, after a presentation of almost 40 minutes, students were filing out of the classroom. One of them said: "Frankly, I have no idea what that presentation was about!" Another student agreed and added: "Why didn't Mrs Smith just cut them off?"

Emily and Isabella were motivated, did a lot of research, and had a great handout. So how could their presentation go so terribly wrong? Of course, they could have rehearsed their presentation at home with a timer. They should also have shortened their presentation right away when they arrived at four pages of handout instead of one – but do you really believe they did not know their presentation would be much longer? What is more plausible is a scenario in which they knew, but simply decided to go along with it, trusting that Mrs Smith would not just cut them off. The question is why.

Having read loads of secondary sources and spent weeks on preparation, Emily and Isabella had a good grasp of their material. They knew how to develop good arguments and support them in a convincing way. Both received top grades for the research papers based on their unlucky presentations. The problem was that they never considered their audience. Having a lot more background on their topic than the other students in the class, they had, at least to some extent, become 'experts' on vampire literature. Telling their classmates just the basics seemed too trivial for an important presentation that might shape the supervisor's opinion of them and their work. That is why they fell in love with the little details – an obscure text on vampires here, a postcolonial analysis there, artfully arranged with the random anecdote on how Lord Byron and his doctor John Polidori fell out with one another about a curious case of plagiarism.[2] The trouble is: that was not what the other students in the seminar needed. Supervisors usually ask students to introduce a topic which will be covered in detail later, or to give a short overview of a topic that is relevant in the context of the seminar, but cannot be covered in detail. As many students will later write a paper based on their course presentations, scholarly standards (such as proper citation and paraphrasing, academic style and register) apply.

What distinguishes a presentation from a research paper, however, is the didactic presentation of the material. Content should be understood by students who are not familiar with the topic, that is why longer quotations and complex facts should be on your handout or otherwise visualized. You are

---

[2]    If this has made you curious, you may want to have a look at Patricia L. Skarda,"Vampirism and Plagiarism: Byron's Influence and Polidori's Practice". *Studies in Romanticism* 28.2 (1989): 249-269. Web. 19 August 2019. <https://www.jstor.org/stable/25600775>.

expected to simplify and take shortcuts in arguments which have to be discussed in detail in your written work. Focus on what your audience needs to follow your train of thought. Make your presentation memorable – not because you were the only one to talk for forty minutes, but because you managed to have everyone's attention for ten.

Begin by writing down the most important goals of your presentation, starting from the state of knowledge your audience already has. What texts have they read? Which definitions are already familiar from previous course meetings, and which ones will you have to introduce? Your goals should be feasible. Isabella and Emily focused on a goal that was not realistic to begin with: to give a complete overview of all vampire literature in English and compare it with contemporary writing from all over the world. It would have been a better goal to focus on the characteristics of vampire literature in its heyday, the late nineteenth century, and then move on to contemporary varieties of the theme, choosing one or two examples. Whatever information you are trying to give in a ten-minute presentation, it can never be exhaustive anyway. What you can do is to make your audience remember the take-home message of your presentation. Observe the rule: "Make things as simple as possible, but not simpler".[3]

You will not look more professional by bombarding the audience with academic jargon and random facts they have no chance of remembering. You can show your professionalism by being well-prepared for background questions, or by looking up proper names and their pronunciation. If you accidentally turn "Georg Lukács" into "George Lucas", you will

---

[3]    This is a paraphrase of the following statement of Albert Einstein: "It can scarcely be denied that the supreme goal of all theory is to make the irreducible basic elements as simple and as few as possible without having to surrender the adequate representation of a single datum of experience". Albert Einstein, "On the Method of Theoretical Physics". *Philosophy of Science*, 1.2 (1934): 163-9, 165 <http://www.jstor.org/stable/184387>.

conjure up Ewoks and lightsabres in your audience's minds instead of studies on the historical novel. And then there was the student who talked about the famous British philosopher [ˈælbət ˈkeɪməs]… who was, of course, none other than French Existentialist [alˈbɛːʁ kaˈmy] (Albert Camus).

Keep an eye on the needs of your audience during the presentation. Timing is an essential part of it. Presentations which are too lengthy cause background noise and impatience in the audience. Your talking speed is something you cannot control directly, it is part of your temperament. Instead of trying to speak considerably slower than your natural speed, speak loudly and clearly. Avoid standing with your back to the audience. Add frequent pauses to let your words sink in.

Look at their faces when you are explaining a complex topic. If they look confused, it is ok to check quickly if they are still following.

Involving your audience is perfectly alright as long as you do not lose too much time. The bigger the audience, the less interaction will be possible. When you ask someone from the audience to read a passage from a slide, do not wait for two minutes until you have a volunteer, but kindly ask someone who is likely to be ok with it. Try not to ask the shy student in the back row who is always embarrassed about his or her accent and may be uncomfortable with being involved unexpectedly. When you ask your audience for associations or impressions during your presentation, do not start a complex discussion, just collect three or four short statements and carry on with your concept. If you need more presentation time because you want to do something interactive, talk to your supervisor first so they can plan ahead.

In a seminar, your audience will probably be respectful. After all, they have been or will be in the same situation as you, so they will want to be helpful and friendly. It is highly unlikely that your fellow students or your supervisor will, on purpose, try to embarrass you or ask you questions you cannot answer. Learn to appreciate the question and answer session after your presentation. If people ask you questions, it is a sign of their attention and genuine interest in your topic. You cannot really prepare for questions, but you should be informed about the period, genre, and author of your text so you have a bit of background knowledge that is not in your presentation. Be patient and polite even if people ask you to clarify something you have already said. You can counter a critical question with limited approval ("yes, but"…): Q: "Milton's Satan is very brave and ready to sacrifice himself for the fallen angels who follow him. Isn't Satan really the hero of *Paradise Lost*?" A: "I agree that Milton ascribes many positive character traits to Satan, but you mustn't forget that he blames God and Eve for Adam's fall, never himself. That's why I think he is motivated by pride, not by true heroism." This way, you acknowledge the other argument, but still stand your ground after your presentation.

If someone asks you a question you have no idea about, that is not a problem. You are a student after all, no one expects you to know as much as your professors. One elegant way is to thank the questioner for bringing that up, admitting that you have not come across that idea yet, but are definitely going to look into that for your research paper (writing it down adds emphasis to the sincerity of your plan to go back to that question later).

There may, however, be situations in which you are faced with a bored or downright hostile audience, for example, if you give a presentation at a student conference which is open to the public. The hostility or boredom may have nothing to do with you in the first place. The person asking a host of critical questions may just have a bad day, or feel obliged but annoyed to be there for reasons not about you at all. Personal commentary after presentations is rare. You may just ignore it or react in a humorous way:

Q: "I almost fell asleep during your presentation, *Hamlet* is so boring!"

A: "I'll tell William Shakespeare the next time I see him!"

Why not simply do the unexpected – agree! "That is exactly what I thought before I had read the play closely. Now I know that there are many interesting scenes, for example…"

If a question is provocative – "Your arguments didn't convince me at all!" –, ask the questioner to clarify: "Could you please give me more details? What was it exactly that you didn't find convincing?"

Do not be afraid of controversial discussions – they are a sure sign that you managed to catch the attention of your audience and reached them emotionally with your talk.

## 4.2 You

You have already analyzed the needs and attitudes of your audience. To arrive at a good rapport with your audience, you are now going to explore your own attitude towards yourself as a presenter. In a way, presenting is like being on stage at a theatre. There are different kinds of people with different personalities contributing to the success of a play. Not all of them are born actors. Which of them are you?

Note: All these types apply to both men and women, regardless of the pronouns used.

### Type 1: The stage hand

Without the stage hand, there would never be a performance, no prop would be in its place. Stage hands are well-organized, reliable, and modest. They think of everything. Their weakness is that they are often rather shy. They prefer not being on stage, unseen, unheard. People looking at them as they stand in front of a course is their nightmare. As presenters, they suffer from stage fright, speak in an all too quiet voice, with a reserved and careful body language, and are happy when it is over.

**Advice:** Stage hands should play on their strengths, which are good preparation and time management. If you can, go to see the room in advance. Bring all cables you might need to attach your own laptop. Are there any speakers, is the volume turned up? Who has a key to the room or any closets you require? How is the lighting in the room? Are there blinds that can be drawn, can the ceiling lights be dimmed, is there a reading light where you stand? When you know that you are so well-prepared nothing can go wrong, your stage fright will bother you much less.

Why start with the leading role? In the weeks before your presentation, other students will be speaking. Begin by asking a question after each presentation. Volunteer to present group work in the course. Or just volunteer to read a text aloud. When you are at the supermarket, be the first person to ask for a second checkout. Given a bit of time, you will get used to people looking at and listening to you.

### Type 2: The lighting technician

The strength of lighting technicians is that they know about effects: everyone loves illumination and a bit of pyrotechnics. When the lights are on, the audience knows that the play is about to begin. The lighting technician has their absolute attention.

The trouble is, the effect evaporates soon, especially when lighting technicians end up illuminating, most of all, themselves. After a while, they are trying to blind the spectators, who cannot see the play they came for, and it does not take long until they are absolutely annoyed.

As presenters, lighting technician start out well, with an unexpected effect, anecdote or story that gains them a laugh from the audience. They have taken classes in rhetorics and know the ropes in their subjects. Unfortunately, their presentation is not interesting enough to keep everyone's attention. They do not care they are blinding the audience with incomprehensible academic jargon or expect them to know the latest theories of an obscure school of French philosophers even the professor has not heard about yet. Watching the technician's presentation is like watching a play for two hours, with the spotlight shining right into your face. You are bored because you cannot follow, and you are irritated and feel uncomfortable. In the end, the lighting technician gets a modest round of polite applause.

**Advice:** Keep up the good effects for grabbing attention. When you prepare your manuscript or notes at home, however, think about what your audience may or may not need. Most importantly, never think of a presentation as routine, something that must be done, and that is always done the same way. Change your approaches, change your methods. Rehearse your presentation with a partner who has no idea about your topic, and manage to interest them. Your presentation will come alive with variety, the unexpected, not by going through every single step as you would go through a shopping-list.

## Type 3: The playwright

When you meet playwrights in real life after reading from one of their plays, you tend to be surprised because you thought they would be taller. They may not be the best actors and actresses, nor the most charismatic personalities. They do not mind people looking at them as long as they have got their script, and everything goes according to plan. They are a little nervous about improvising and always think they could have done better if they had done more editing. Their magic, however, unfolds in their stories. When they start talking, the audience goes quiet and everyone listens.

Playwrights are not born presenters (they may be a bit clumsy, so they should keep a glass of water well away from the technical equipment), but they have an eye on the audience. They know what their listeners want: a well-written, creative, and logical presentation of original arguments, presented in a way that will surprise them.

**Advice:** Captivate the audience with a good story – yes, that is possible in academia. Like a good fairy tale, an academic problem starts with a situation in which something is lacking or missing, like Hansel and Gretel being poor and out in the woods alone. It is the hero/heroine of the fairy tale that comes up with an idea to solve the problem, has to overcome many obstacles, tensions, and doubts (like the scholar when his research seems to be a dead end), and finally, the problem is solved. Guide your audience through your story. If you make a mistake, ignore it or gently mend it. Do not apologize profusely for your accent, your outdated computer equipment or for not knowing everything.

## Type 4: The lead

The leads' strength is their charisma. They know the audience love them, and they prove worthy with a well-prepared performance, always keeping the audience attentive and comfortable. They bring across topics with great sincerety and involvement. Leads are spontaneous, know how to improvise, and how to make an entrance. When everyone else has grabbed an old pair of jeans and a white tee from the wardrobe, you may find the actor dressed to the latest fashion or the actress wearing that stunning cobalt blue blazer with matching earrings exactly the colour of her slides. The lead does not have many obvious weaknesses, but they may secretly think they are not as organized as the stage hand, as clever as the playwright, or as self-assured as the lighting technician.

**Advice:** Have a little faith in your expertise as a young researcher. Try out new perspectives, new methods, move outside the comfort zone. Along with your presentation skills, you will be hard to beat. Stop mentally criticizing yourself during the presentation. Two or three days later, you can still go through your notes and summarize for yourself what you have learnt from the presentation: "X and Y went well. The next time I talk about Z, I will …"

## 4.3 Your material

Although nearly everyone has already heard presentations which consisted of nothing but summaries of secondary texts, and although everyone has already been bored to tears and remembered nothing of this type of presentation, the first step many students take in writing their course presentations is – to summarize secondary literature! Their hope is that, by reading the works of their elders and betters, they are eventually going to find out what their topic is all about, "to see if thence would flow / Some fresh and fruitfull showers upon my sunne-burn'd braine".[4] Of course doing research on what has been written about your topic is a necessary step in writing your presentation, however, more importantly, there are two sets of questions which have to precede this:

What do you want to achieve with this presentation? Do you want to introduce your fellow students to a new text,

---

[4]    Sir Philip Sidney,"Loving in Truth" *(Astrophil and Stella 1)*, *The Poems of Sir Philip Sidney*, ed. William Ringler jun. (Oxford: Clarendon, 1962), 165.

author, methodology, theory, approach, a practical skill they should be able to apply? What is the 'message' you want them to take home with them after you stopped talking?

8. How do you achieve this? What didactic, visual, technical etc. tools are you going to use to make your presentation memorable?

When I was in eighth grade, my physics teacher wanted us to learn something about forces. She told us that an item with the mass of 100g corresponded to the force of 1 N. She took a bar of chocolate from her bag and attached it to a spring scale, which measured the force of exactly 1 N. Then we were allowed to share the bar of chocolate among us. I do not remember a lot from eighth-grade physics lessons, but I have never forgotten that a bar of chocolate exerts a force of 1 N. Why? Not because of the chocolate. It was not like 100g divided by 30 people made an awesome amount of chocolate for everyone. I remember the lesson because chocolate was an unusual tool in the physics classroom. Our teacher could have made the same point with metal weights. She managed to link her take-home message ("100g is equivalent to 1 N") with a memorable, unusual event in our minds ("chocolate in school"). As the event was stored in our brains – we may have had chocolate on many other occasions, but never before or again in a physics classroom –, so did the take-home message.

Be creative in your approach to the presentation. Why not use a poster or diorama with small groups, for example to illustrate what an Elizabethan stage looks like? Examples of creative methods are

- imaginary journey (the presenter asks students to close their eyes and imagine they are Shakespeare, looking for a patron),

- pool of ideas (the group freely associate ideas with the key word "Enlightenment"),
- intermediality (approaching Keats' poem "La Belle Dame Sans Merci" by introducing its musical settings by Charles Villiers Stanford and Loreena McKennitt),
- anachronistic approach (look at a current issue of a women's magazine and compare the stereotypical topics with the depiction of women in Jane Austen's novels).

For most presentations, you will be required to submit a handout which summarizes the theses of your presentation. Look at your handout as a didactic tool: it should contain the necessary terminology (with short explanations), your theses, references to secondary literature, and a list of works cited in MLA format. Didactic presentations should progress in a logical order from thesis via explanations to examples. You can present a roadmap at the beginning of your presentation so your audience will know what to expect. Like your research paper, your presentation should have a conclusion. It can highlight further points of discussion. Studies have shown that your audience will remember the first and last parts of your presentation best, whereas the content delivered in the middle is remembered the least.[5] Therefore, it is essential that you do not simply stop your presentation at the last aspect of its content. Summarize, provide a clear message, and finish with a catchy sentence.

---

[5]    Molly Rideout, Melissa Held, Alison Volpe Holmes, "The Didactic Makeover: Keep it Short, Active, Relevant". *Pediatrics* 138.1 (2016): 1. Web. 24 August 2019.
<https://pediatrics.aappublications.org/content/pediatrics/138/1e20160751.full.pdf>.

**Exercises**

### Exercise 4.1: Preparing and Improvising

In the practice part, you are going to look at situations that may go wrong during a presentation. Think about what you may do in advance to prevent this and/or try to improvise as spontaneously as possible.

**Situation 1:** You have prepared the slides for your presentation in Microsoft PowerPoint. When you insert the USB stick, the file cannot be displayed because on the computer at university, an older version of the programme has been installed that is incompatible with your file type.

**Situation 2:** During your presentation, you notice that there is a lot of background noise in the audience. Your fellow students are whispering among themselves, rustling with papers or rummaging in their bags. Others are just looking out of the window.

**Situation 3:** As you are approaching an important aspect of your presentation, the construction workers next door turn on their jackhammer, drowning your words.

**Situation 4:** As you start talking about an aspect of a book that is on your reading list for the course, people's expressions are blank. It starts dawning on you that they may not all have read the novel.

### Exercise 4.2: Questions and Answers

How would you react to the following questions and comments after your presentation?

a) "I liked your presentation, but I have no idea why you chose *Twilight* as a topic. That isn't a good text at all, is it?"

b) "Your arguments didn't convince me at all."
c) "Could you compare the position of that critic you have just presented to E.M. Forster's arguments?" (it goes without saying that you have never heard of E.M. Forster)

# Chapter 5: Writing Abstracts

Before you start writing your text, you should have a plan of how to proceed and what to achieve. An abstract is a short description of your later research project. It outlines the focus of your thesis as well as the methods you are going to use to approach your topic. You do not need to have any results at this stage, but you can point out possible solutions.

Abstracts are also frequently required in academia if you want to speak at a conference or write a contribution for a volume of essays. This is the first impression of your work for the organizers of a congress or the editor of a book.

The advantage of writing abstracts is that you are compelled to think about how you would like to approach your topic at an early stage. If you provide such a brief description in advance, any methodological weaknesses or dangers can be identified and corrected in the planning phase without any deductions in assessment.

## 5.1 Structure of an Abstract

A meaningful checklist for elements an abstract should comprise is provided by Philip Koopman.[1] For the purposes of this book addressed to students and other writers of research papers in the humanities, the descriptions of the structural elements have been modified accordingly:

---

[1]  The following list of structuring elements follows Philip Koopman, "How to Write an Abstract". *Electrical and Computer Engineering, Carnegie Mellon University.* Web. 19 August 2019. <http://www.ece.cmu.edu/~koopman/essays/abstract.html>.

- **Motivation**
  The first paragraph of your abstract clarifies your motivation. Why should your readers bother with this topic at all? It is not enough that your topic is "interesting" for you or that you need a good grade. Explain the relevance of your topic in a broader context. The fact that no one else has written about it yet may not be enough (it might just mean that the topic is irrelevant to the field). Say why there is a gap in the existing research on the topic, and how your study is going to fill it. You do not have to construct a real-world relevance that will change society forever, such as finding a cure for cancer or solving the millennium problems in mathematics, but there should be a theoretical, methodological or practical gain which you highlight in your abstract, a contribution to an already existing discussion; Catherine Baker suggests to think of an abstract as a kind of 'narrative' which you have to move forward towards a problem.[2]
- **Problem statement**
  What problem do you intend to solve? What are the limits of your study? Avoid saying what you are NOT going to do.
- **Approach**
  Which method do you want to use to solve the problem? Are you going to study reception theory by handing out fifty questionnaires on a book to your fellow students? Are you going to do archival work? Would you like to explore relations between two texts by applying Kristeva's concept of intertextuality? Are you analyzing time in three different novels by means of narrative theory or had you rather refer

---

[2]    See also Catherine Baker, "How to Write a Conference Abstract: A Five-Part Plan for Pitching Your Research at Almost Anything". *University of Hull*. Web. 19 August 2019. <https://bakercatherine.wordpress.com/2017/03/15/how-to-write-a-conference-abstract-a-five-part-plan-for-pitching-your-research-at-almost-anything/>.

to Bakhtin's chronotope? Which theoretical frameworks do you intend to use? Think carefully about which methods will contribute most to solving your problem, and which ones are appropriate to your research questions.

- **Theses**
  What claims will you make? What should your arguments be based on?
- **(optional) Conclusions, implications**
  What results do you expect? What conclusions can you possibly draw from your work, once it is finished?

Apart from adhering roughly to this structure, you can improve your abstract by avoiding the following mistakes:

- **Colloquial language** ("don't", "can't", "And it's…", "But it's…"). In an academic style and register, you would not use any contractions, nor start sentences with "And" or "But".
- **Direct questions** ("Is it really true that *The Book of Dave* is a satire?"). Since direct questions are associated with spoken language, reported speech is preferable in written form ("The question arises whether *The Book of Dave* can really be considered a satire").
- **Personal opinion** ("I think…", "In my opinion", "I like…"). Scientific work is not about expressing your subjective feelings. Assert views that are based on fact, scientific research, and argumentation.
- **Empty phrases** ("It is interesting", "This would go beyond the scope of this paper"). As a motivation, it is neither enough that your topic is exciting for you, nor that no one has researched it so far – go on to explain the relevance of your question. The fact that you cannot offer an exhaustive discussion of Shakespeare's complete works in ten to twelve pages is not worth mentioning either.

- **Historical and biographical information without sense and purpose** ("John Keats was a great Romantic poet"). If you mention such details in your work, this should not be done to fill pages, but to contextualize your work in literary history. If historical and biographical information does not contribute to the solution of your problem, it should not be part of your paper.

- **Summaries and retellings of your primary text** ("Emily travels through the Pyrenees with her father and falls in love with Valancourt. Then her father dies and she becomes the ward of her aunt, who will not permit her to marry…"). For abstracts and term papers, assume an informed peer group as your readership – these are readers with a general academic background, but without special knowledge, so that you can assume they know the "tools of the trade" (such as terms like 'metaphor' or 'narrator') and have read all primary texts.

## 5.2 Example

### The Mythification of History through Story-Telling in Adam Thorpe's *Hodd* (2009)

The changing perception of history as philosophy of history emphasizes the transformation and reconstruction of the historical source in the processs of its reception by the historian – an approach that implies a high degree of productivity and appears to view historiography as a creative act, as an art rather than a "hard science".

**Motivation:** mnemonic turn has changed perceptions of history, stories become more important

With this mnemonic turn, totalitarian modes of presentation are replaced by the realization that the past can only be accessed through the stories told about it.

**The questions of how individuals or nations remember their own past, how they document that past in the form of narratives and deal with matters of memory and recollection have greatly influenced contemporary English literature. Not only traditional modes of narration, but also classical myths of England, its folklore and its heroes are called into question.**

**Problem statement:** the contemporary historical novel calls traditional notions of the past into question

Such approaches which challenge traditional notions of history are Foucault's discourse theory or New Historicism, as to be seen in the writings of Stephen Greenblatt and Hayden White.

**Method:** discourse theory, New Historicism

This case study is going to look at the changing perception of one of England's most wide-spread myths, Robin Hood, from the early sources over the romanticized image of Sir Walter Scott's *Ivanhoe* and its countless adaptations into television, cinema and

**Approach:** case study of Robin Hood myth

popular culture to the villainous type of character of Adam Thorpe's 2009 novel *Hodd*.

With every generation adding to it, the story of the famous English outlaw exemplifies one of the central ideas of the mnemonic turn to historiography – that there can never be one historical „truth", but many.

**Theses:**
– perceptions of Robin Hood change
– there is not one historical truth, but many

Reduce your abstracts to the essentials. If you have a chance to discuss your abstract with the lecturer, please take notes – you will receive important feedback on potential weaknesses of the finished paper.

## Exercises

### Exercise 5: Improving an Abstract
Examine the following example for strengths and weaknesses.

### Betrayal in Blake Morrison's *The Last Weekend*
With the character of Iago in *Othello*, Shakespeare created a prototypical villain whose name has become synonymous with betrayal. However, except for some obscure hints on promotion or jealousy, Iago's motivation remains in the dark. In his gripping 2010 novel *The Last Weekend*, Blake Morrison gives a voice to Iago's 21st-century counterpart, Ian, a married primary school teacher who's invited by his snobbish university friend Ollie for a country weekend. Ian strives to establish a bond with the reader. Yet a thinly-disguised agenda of self-justification questions Ian's reliability even before intertextual

evidence links him to Iago, raising the suspicions of readers that they are about to be 'betrayed' themselves. Slowly, but steadily, Ian's mask of integrity begins to slip. Thus the reader asks himself: Why does Ian betray both his friend Ollie and the reader, and how is the motif of betrayal linked to Shakespeare's drama?

Echoes of Shakespeare's *Othello* pervade Morrison's novel: the names of the protagonists, Ian, Ollie, Daisy, Emily, a telltale tissue, a plot driven by betrayal and jealousy-induced murder – close enough to evoke its literary predecessor, independent enough to surprise with an unexpected ending.

In Morrison's novel, those who betray do so because they have reached an impasse in their career and personal development. They are haunted by the realization that "you're stuck with who you are till you cease to be" (252). Ian's concluding words, "I'm a survivor", are true in the literal sense – but survival also implies the betrayer's failure to let his old self die and be re-born. In this paper, I am going to show that *The Last Weekend* is not a simple re-working of *Othello*, but a parody of the self-betrayal of the British middle class at the close of the New Labour reign. Society's growing demands that everyone has to achieve status and luxury to be considered 'successful' are likely to promote narcissistic personalities and to lower inhibitions, which makes people prone to betrayal when their ambitions are at stake.

# Chapter 6: Academic Texts

When choosing secondary texts you are going to use for your research paper, you will be confronted with several types of academic texts which differ not only in length, but also in terms of timeliness, status, and, quite possibly, accuracy and quality. This chapter illustrates the features of academic texts intended for publication, which you will need to support your arguments, or to research a topic in detail for coursework and exams, such as monograph, research article, and review. You will learn how to select useful materials and assess their accuracy and impact.

## 6.1 Types of Academic Texts

### Monograph

A monograph is a book about one topic (author, genre, period, aspect), usually by one author. Dissertations or 'second books' written for the purpose of additional academic qualification in the humanities are still typically monographs, but not all monographs fall into that category. The advantage of monographs as sources for academic papers is the wealth of material, as monographs tend to have at least 200 pages. The author is an expert on his chosen topic. The form and degree of quality control varies by publisher. There are two types of academic publishers: 1) vanity publisher: the author pays for having his book published, 2) trade or general interest publisher: the author does not have to pay for publishing his book. The risk of failure is the publisher's. A monograph published with a vanity publisher has not normally been peer-reviewed (*i.e.* read, criticized and recommended for publication by other experts in the field), but its quality has been assessed by examiners and supervisors if the book was written for academic qualification. A monograph with a trade or general interest publisher has frequently been peer-reviewed and/or approved by the editorial board, as well as proofread and optimized professionally by an editor.

As it takes relatively long to write and publish a monograph, however, some of the information you find there may not be up to date when you locate it. Additionally, you see the topic through the lens of a single author. Therefore, a monograph should never be the only source of information on your topic.

## Edited Volume

Edited volumes include articles by different authors, either from the same discipline or interdisciplinary collaboration, preceded by an introduction by one or more editors. Frequently, there is an occasion for publishing an edited volume, such as conference proceedings, the contributions of a lecture series, or as a *festschrift* for a respected colleague. **Conference proceedings** (or special issues of a scholarly journal published in collaboration with the organizing team of the congress) tend to reflect the latest state of the art in a given discipline, whereas other types of edited volumes may take years to become available in print. Contributions in edited volumes have been reviewed by a board of editors.

## Article in an Academic Journal, Online Journal

Academic journals are the medium of exchange within the scientific community in medicine and the natural sciences. The reason for this is the relatively fast process of publication, as compared to publishing books. Journals can be monthly, quarterly, biennial, or annual, so they tend to reflect the state of the art in a given discipline – at least theoretically. In practice, an author may be asked to revise and resubmit his article several times, or apply to several papers before it is accepted. The practice of peer-review is an established means of quality control, however, one must not forget that there is a publishing industry behind academic journals. Therefore, decisions may be influenced by other factors and interests as well. Some open-access journals may publish an article with little or no quality control if the author is willing to pay for publication (these are sometimes referred to as "predatory presses"). Having been published without any quality control, however, does not automatically imply that an article is not academic. It is relatively difficult for an inexperienced writer of research papers to see the difference and thus judge the quality of a journal or article. The best course of action is to turn to your local library when in doubt.[1]

## Article in a Handbook, Dictionary, Encyclopaedia, or Lexicon

In a handbook, you will find relatively short articles which provide a general overview of a given topic, such as an author's biography, a branch of literary theory, a 'school' of philosophy, or a current cultural trend or 'turn'. You can quote from a handbook in your written work if you are looking for a general definition or a first introduction to the topic. If the term, however, is seminal to your writing, you will require additional literature focusing exclusively on the aspects important for your topic. When quoting a handbook or lexicon article, ensure your bibliographic record is complete, listing not only the editor(s) of the handbook, but also the author of

---

[1]    "Predatory Open Access Publishers". FAU University Library. Web. 25 August 2019. <https://ub.fau.de/en/writing-publishing/open-access/predatory-open-access-publishers/>.

the individual article. In handbooks, the authors of individual articles are usually abbreviated by their initals. A list is provided at the beginning or the end of the handbook.

## Review

In science, a "review" is an article which provides a summary or overview of the state of research on a given topic. In the humanities, "review" refers to the judgment passed on the quality of a text or cultural artefact (a novel, a theatre performance, but also a monograph or edited volume) by a professional critic or expert in the field.[2]

Reviews can be very revealing as to how a book was received when it was published. Use reviews published in quality papers (not customer reviews on the websites of publishers or booksellers). The views expressed, however, are the subjective impression of the author of the review. They are not normally substantiated by academic evidence. Given the fast-paced world of news, it is not even a sure fact that the reviewer has read or understood the entire book. You should treat statements made in reviews with caution. Critical evaluation of the material is more important with the review than with any other type of source. If you observe these basics, however, comparing several reviews can tell you a lot about how other people have perceived the text and will provide you with a different perspective. Especially when you are writing a research paper on a recently published book, it may take a while for academic text types on your primary texts to become available.

---

[2]    Please note that in English, a "literary critic" is someone who analyses literature professionally in an academic context (German: Literaturwissenschaftler), whereas someone who writes an article about a new novel in a newspaper, assessing whether it is, as Oscar Wilde put it, "well-written or badly written", is a "reviewer" (German: "Literaturkritiker").

**Academic Blog**

Many people share their thoughts and their lives in a blog (derived from 'web log'). The advantage of a blog over a traditional website is that content can be added from any place in the world with an internet connection, you do not require any additional software (such as website editors or FTP upload tools). Readers can comment on a blog article directly. To be considered an academic blog that can be quoted in papers, the same rules apply as with other online sources: blog posts adhere to good academic practice, the authors and editors have academic qualifications, and the blog exercises some form of quality control (not all blogs are peer-reviewed). An example for academic blogging in the humanities and the social sciences is the European blogging platform https://hypotheses.org/, provided by Open Edition, a French forum for digital publishing supported by the *Centre National de la Recherche Scientifique*. *Hypotheses.org* offers portals in English, French, German, and Spanish.

## 6.2 Evaluating Academic Texts

So you have used library catalogues, bibliographies, other databases, and specialized search engines. You have been to the libraries available to you, ordered books via interlibrary loan, and photocopies of articles with a document delivery service. You have grouped the materials available to you into different types of texts and know what to expect from each type. Still you are faced with an embarrassment of riches: which texts are really going to be useful to you in writing your paper? Reading the abstract (if available), a review of a monograph, or the article itself is just the first step. One of the criteria your supervisor is going to look at when grading your paper is how you evaluated sources.

**Timeliness.** Is your source state-of-the-art in its field? This may be a hard question to answer, especially for a beginning student. You have no way of knowing the latest trends in a field you have only just entered. Your best guess is the time of publication as well as the medium of publication. Articles published in journals are usually more current than mono-graphs, conference proceedings reflect trends and recent developments in the field, whereas blog entries usually show a glimpse of works in progress and ideas to come. Do not use any publications older than 15 years, unless they are absolutely standard – Roland Barthes published his seminal article "The Death of the Author" back in 1967, but it is still a much-discussed text you are very welcome to quote in your paper (as long as you show that you are aware of the developments in literary criticism since the 1960s, such as the fact that Seán Burke devoted an entire book to *The Death and Return of the Author* in 2010). There is no guarantee, of course, that a recently published article will reflect the current state of research, nor that young scholars will have progressive views. Try turning the tables though: a book on gender roles published in the 1950s is highly unlikely to be of help in a paper on contemporary feminist novelists.

**Matching.** Does the source do anything to support your line of argument? That does not mean the author has to share your views. A contradictory opinion may also be very useful to look at the topic from different angles. What is meant by matching, however, is that you should view your topic as a sieve. When you pour the source through that sieve, will you distil something useful out of the whole process? If the source is just fascinating because it explores an original topic or because it is well-written and contains many quotable phrases – forget about it. Anything that distracts your reader (your supervisor) from the topic and from the brilliance of your own interpretation should be discarded.

**Substantiation of Claims.** It goes without saying that the quality of an academic text relies on how well claims are substantiated. Is the line of argument logical? Have causes and effects been clarified? Which sources have been used, how are they evaluated? Does the author use appropriate examples? Are the claims plausible considering the primary text(s)?

**Language.** A source you are going to use in your writing at university should be written in academic register, avoiding not only colloquialisms and dialect, but also polemics and irony. Furthermore, terminology should be used unequivocally and correctly. Scholarly writing should promote learning – clear, concise language is the distinctive trademark of a 'good' academic text.

## 6.3 Text Types in Student Writing

Now you have familiarized yourself with the types of sources you may want to use for your written coursework, it is time to get down to writing. Although the research paper is the most common form of assessment in some contexts, such as the candidature for a degree, it may not be the only type of writing you do during your studies. Writing tasks vary a lot between countries, as you may find out when studying abroad for a year or more. Whereas countries in Southern Europe, such as Italy or Spain, often limit student assessment to answering exam questions, research papers are written by undergraduates in Germany from their second year of study, whereas in the UK, it is quite common to submit two to three essays per course instead of one long paper at the end of the year. This chapter serves as a general introduction to what types of writing may be expected of you, starting with genres of a varying degree of formality such as reading responses and essays, as opposed to more formalized texts such as the research paper or thesis.

## Abstract

An abstract is a short summary 1) of a paper you are planning to write, or 2) of an article in a scholarly journal. Abstracts contain the motivation for the paper, a problem statement, the methodology used, as well as tentative conclusions or goals. For advice on how to write an abstract, see Chapter 5.

## Reading Response, Reader Response Paper

In contrast to other forms of academic writing, reading responses do not require you to do research and look for secondary sources. What a reading response documents is that you have read and understood the text and are able to explain how you perceived elements central to the text (for example, narrative strategy, treatment of class, race, gender). Back up your arguments with evidence from the text. You do not need a long introduction, you start with the question right away and sum up your ideas with a brief but concise conclusion. Zachary Schrag illustrates the purpose of the reading response quite vividly: "A reading response is not like the commentary track on a DVD, in which a director watches the film and says whatever pops into his mind. If anything, it is more like a trailer for the film, in which short clips are presented in a new order, for another result".[3]

---

[3]    Zachary Schrag,"How to Write a Reading Response". *HistoryProfessor.Org*. Web. 02 September 2019. <https://historyprofessor.org/reading/how-to-write-a-reading-response/>.

**Example – Reading Response Question:**

In popular culture, the creature in Mary Shelley's *Frankenstein* (1818) is frequently referred to as a 'monster'. Do you consider this assessment appropriate? Write 250 words.

The creature in Mary Shelley's *Frankenstein* (1818) is monstrous in terms of its looks. Victor Frankenstein assembled it from body parts, selecting only those he considered beautiful, however, his creature turns out to be horrible: "His yellow skin scarcely covered the work of muscles and arteries beneath; […] his teeth of a pearly whiteness; but these luxuriances only formed a more horrid contrast with his watery eyes, that seemed almost of the same colour as the dun-white sockets in which they were set, his shrivelled complexion and straight black lips" (32). With 8 foot in height, it is taller and than the average human being. When Frankenstein abandons the creature, it is obsessed by revenge and acts monstrously, killing innocents such as William and Elizabeth (136-137). That is, however, only one aspect of its character. The creature displays human emotions, such as suffering and loneliness: "I am malicious because I am miserable. Am I not shunned and hated by all mankind?" (98). The creature demands a companion because it is shunned by human beings because of its looks, as the example of the deLacey family illustrates. Although the creature feels compassion for the impoverished family and tries to help them, they reject it as soon as they see it for the first time. Therefore, the assessment of the creature as a monster is only partly correct, as Frankenstein refuses to take responsibility for his creation and thus behaves in a monstrous way himself, abandoning his creature and lying to his friends and family to disguise his unethical behaviour.

Mary Shelley, *Frankenstein. The 1818 Text*. Ed. Paul Hunter. New York: Norton, 2012.

This reading response does not cite or paraphrase any secondary literature. Unlike in an essay or in a research paper, you do not have to define what a 'monster' or 'monstrous' is, nor do you have to give evidence for size being a distinctive feature of many literary monsters. A reading response is about your understanding of the text. It does, however, quote from and refer to the primary text. You should indicate the edition you used for later reference.

## Essay

First of all, one should distinguish between an essay as a literary genre or mode of writing, and an academic essay as a form of assessment in a programme of study. Essayistic texts in literature, as they were written by Michel de Montaigne, Sir Francis Bacon, Joseph Addison, or Samuel Johnson, are open and associative in form, looking at a given topic from many different angles. They do not follow formal rules or assert definitive views.

The essay is a form of assessment popular in anglophone countries. A list of essay questions to choose from is normally provided by the lecturer or professor. What differentiates an academic essay from a research paper is not only its length – you may hand in two to three essays of 2,000 words each to pass a course, but only one research paper –, but also its structure. Essays are not structured as formally in terms of a table of contents, chapters, and headlines as research papers usually are. Too much meandering, however, is also detrimental to academic essays because the golden thread and logical reasoning of your line of argument should be recognizable at any point. In essays, students should demonstrate that they are able to discuss a complex topic and organize their ideas. An essay should have an introduction which explains the focus of the essay, and a conclusion which should respond to the issues raised in the introduction.

The focus of an essay is narrow in comparison to a research paper. Students are expected to do some research and cite or paraphrase sources to back up their ideas, but a comprehensive understanding of the topic is not required; select the material most relevant to solving the problem. If required, literature reviews that reflect the current state of research on the topic can be kept brief.

**Example – Essay Question:**

How does Stevenson explore the theme of duality in *Strange Case of Dr Jekyll and Mr Hyde* (1886)? Write 1500 words.

When Henry Jekyll, the main character of Robert Louis Stevenson's *Strange Case of Dr Jekyll and Mr Hyde* (1886), eventually tells his story, he admits to being "committed to a profound duplicity of life" (48). The theme of duality is explored by Stevenson in the form of the duality of individual identity, as the darker side of Jekyll's personality manifests in his alter ego Edward Hyde. In addition to that, the short novel also illustrates the duality of Victorian society caused by moral conformity, and the duality of human nature in terms of Darwin's discovery of evolution, presenting Hyde as the "troglodyte" who is only thinly veiled by civilization.

The 'split personality' of Jekyll and Hyde shows that identity is always characterized by duality. No human being can be entirely good or evil. Jekyll is a "double dealer" (48) long before he takes his drug for the first time. He does not merely attempt to be respected in public, but he feels compelled to "wear a *more than commonly* grave countenance" (*ibid*.), to be morally superior, more saintly than everyone else. Jekyll thus discloses his secret hubris, his desire to be raised above his fellow men.

Hyde is human, as he is a part of Jekyll, but at the same time, he is excessively different (Smith, *Gothic Radicalism*, 171). Thus

Hyde cannot be fully interpreted, as the description by Enfield shows:

> He is not easy to describe. There is something wrong with his appearance; something displeasing, something downright detestable. I never saw a man I so disliked, and yet I scarce know why. He must be deformed somewhere; he gives a strong feeling of deformity, although I couldn't specify the point. He's an extraordinary-looking man, and yet I really can name nothing out of the way. No, sir; I can make no hand of it; I can't describe him. And it's not want of memory; for I declare I can see him this moment (11-12).

Enfield is emotionally overwhelmed by meeting Hyde and yet he is incapable of a full interpretation of what he is seeing because Hyde is also closely linked to notions of the Satanic. Jekyll himself cannot help feeling some "sympathy for the devil": Hyde is "much less exercised, much less exhausted […], smaller, slighter and younger" than Jekyll, "natural and human […], it bore a livelier image of the spirit, it seemed more express and single, than the imperfect and divided countenance I had been hitherto accustomed to call mine" (51). As Twitchell observes, "Hyde is almost Jekyll as a teenager, the 'Jekyll' that Dr. Jekyll has had to repress to become, like Utterson, a man of property, a man of means" (237). As a 'teenage version' of Jekyll, Hyde does not have to worry about reputation or sustenance – like a concerned parent, Jekyll has taken precautions and made Hyde his heir in case of his sudden disappearance; as Jekyll confesses, "[m]en have before hired bravos to transact their crimes […]. I was the first that ever did so for his pleasures" (52). It is this selfish motive that Jekyll ultimately holds responsible for his failure, not having approached his endeavour "with a more noble spirit" (51). Stevenson's shift in narrative perspective contributes to the impression of duality, as the previous chapters have created a bias against Jekyll, however, the high potential for identification that is inherent in a first-person narrative perspective invites the narratee to empathize with Jekyll's pain. Meanwhile, Jekyll is still lying to himself, claiming his experiment might have turned out differently had he approached it with less selfish intentions (51). In this way, the narratee is drawn into the duality of Jekyll's personality.

The character of Jekyll/Hyde is, however, not merely used to illustrate the duality of the individual, comprising 'good' and 'evil' character traits, but represents the duality of a whole society. Victorian ideology is characterized by a firm belief in outward conformity and respectability (Allingham n.pag.), and one of the worst Victorian nightmares is the loss of dignity.

One of the key concepts when it comes to understanding Victorian thought is respectability. Having witnessed the French Revolution and its time of insecurity and political cruelty, the British lived in fear that a similar upheaval might take place in their country as well (Dawson 18). The reasons for the revolution were seen as moral, not primarily political, so the solution seemed to be a strict moral corset that everyone in the middle or upper classes should adhere to (Dawson 45). Respectability was a code of behaviour which governed every aspect of the lives of the Victorians (Linehan 210): it was essential to upward mobility in society, to wealth and success. It defined acceptable modes of behaviour, language and appearance, comprising social rules and moral conduct. A fear of excess of male sexual desire was paired with a need to restrain it. The inhumane high standards of morality clashed with the reality of Victorian society. Stevenson's novel explores the clash between the need to maintain respectability and the desire to follow one's inclinations:

> And indeed the worst of my faults was a certain impatient gaiety of disposition, such as has made the happiness of many, but such as I found it hard to reconcile with my imperious desire to carry my head high, and wear a more than commonly grave countenance before the public. Hence it came about that I concealed my pleasures; and that

> when I reached years of reflection, and began to look round me and
> take stock of my progress and position in the world, I stood already
> committed to a profound duplicity of life. Many a man would have
> even blazoned such irregularities as I was guilty of; but from the high
> views that I had set before me, I regarded and hid them with an almost
> morbid sense of shame (47-8)

In this passage, Jekyll describes how he is forced to hide his
passions and desires because of the conventions of society.
The fact that Dr Lanyon, the epitome of a respectable Victorian, has been wary of Jekyll's research from the beginning,
emphasizes that Jekyll is correct in his assessment. Giving in
to his inclinations would render him an outcast in Victorian
society. Therefore, Stevenson's treatment of duality can be
read as a criticism of the moral depravity and hypocrisy of
Victorian society, demanding saintly standards impossible to
meet.

At the same time, Darwin's theory of evolution exacer-
bated the conflict between religion and science, a development that strongly affected literature. Since the Italian physi-
ognomist Cesare Lombroso's works, criminals were regarded
as "evolutionary throwbacks" (Gould 133). It was widely be-
lieved that criminals could be recognized easily because they
bore anatomical traits of apes (*ibid*.).

These assumptions are instrumentalized in the text. Hyde
is "smaller, slighter, and younger" (51) than Jekyll. Archaeo-
logical evidence suggests that in the early stages of humanity,
individuals were smaller and slighter, with a lower life expec-
tancy than modern man. Jekyll describes Hyde as "less developed" (51) than his respectable side, which suggests he comes
from a primitive state of human evolution.

This is also in accordance with the impressions by the maid-
servant and Utterson: on several occasions in the short novel,
Hyde is described as ape-like, or as bearing resemblance to a
cave-dweller, *e.g.* "Mr Hyde was pale and dwarfish, he gave
an impression of deformity without any nameable malforma-

tion […] God bless me, the man seems hardly human! Something troglodytic, shall we say?" (17), and "he broke out in a great flame of anger, stamping with his foor, brandishing the cane […], with ape-like fury, he was trampling his victim underfoot, and hailing down a storm of blows" (22). The brutish, savage behaviour of Hyde reflects the fears of Victorian society induced by Darwin's theory of evolution, claiming that men and apes were related in an evolutionary process, implying that civilization was merely a thin veil separating men from beasts. With the fears of the bloody terrors of the Revolution in France still in mind, the idea that man might not be more civilized than an ape if he decided to follow his primitive instincts was terrifying to Stevenson's readers.

All in all, it can be observed that Stevenson approaches the theme of duality from three different dominant perspectives: firstly, the duplicity of the individual. Jekyll's ruin, however, is not presented as the result of his having a dark side, but as a consequence of pretending he did not. Secondly, the strong role of public opinion and respectability in Jekyll's reflections reveals the duality of Victorian society, whose members feel obliged to hide their true opinions to succeed in their careers and be regarded with respect by their friends and neighbours. Thirdly, by associating Hyde with a proto-human stage of evolution, Stevenson's short novel mirrors the fears of society of the hidden aggression and duality within human nature, which the progress-oriented Victorians had a hard time accepting.

### List of Works Cited

Allingham, "Victorian Earnestness". *The Victorian* Web. Web.18 August 2019. <http://www.victorianweb.org/vn/pva97.html>.

Dawson, Gowen. *Darwin, Literature and Victorian Respectability*. Cambridge: CUP, 2007. Print.

Gould, Stephen Jay. "Post-Darwinist Theories of the Ape Within". Robert Louis Stevenson, *Strange Case of Dr Jekyll and Mr Hyde*, ed. Katherine Linehan. New York: Norton, 2003. 132-133. Print.

Linehan, Katherine. "Sex, Secrecy and Self-Alienation in *Strange Case of Dr Jekyll and Mr Hyde*". Robert Louis Stevenson, *Strange Case of Dr Jekyll and Mr Hyde*, ed. Katherine Linehan. New York: Norton, 2003. 204-214. Print.

Stevenson, Robert Louis. *Strange Case of Dr Jekyll and Mr Hyde*, ed. Katherine Linehan. New York: Norton, 2003. Print.

Twitchell, James B. *Dreadful Pleasures. An Anatomy of Modern Horror*. Oxford: OUP, 1985. Print.

As you can see, an essay uses secondary literature, quotes and paraphrases of other academics' thoughts correctly in MLA style, and gives evidence for any claims made. It also has a short list of works cited. The introduction contains a few hints to the structure of your argument, as you will not normally provide a table of contents, nor will you separate the parts of your essay by headlines. Guide your reader through the structure of your essay by using words such as "therefore", "furthermore", "subsequently".

## Research Paper

The topic of a research paper is more abstract than that of an essay. Whereas students normally pick an essay question from a list provided in class, they are asked to propose a topic for a research paper themselves. Along with logical reasoning and discussion, a research paper assesses also the academic skills students have developed over the semester. Are you able to locate resources at the library or in a database? Are you capable of evaluating these sources critically? Have you developed a comprehensive overview of the state of research on your topic? Can you draw abstract conclusions from your topic? Have you presented your findings in academic language? Have you mastered the conventions of style in your field? Towards the end of your studies: have you developed an original approach to your topic that contributes something new to the discussions already pending?

When your research paper becomes a thesis to obtain a degree at the end of your studies, two aspects become more important: time management, and level of abstraction. Writing a longer text of 40 (BA) to 100 (MA) pages requires more planning than a ten-page term paper in an undergraduate seminar. Furthermore, you will be expected to be more independent from secondary literature, develop original claims, and draw more abstract conclusions from concrete examples than it is the case in your previous written asssigents.

**Example – Research Paper Topic:**
Studies on the Role of the *Doppelgänger* Motif in Robert Louis Stevenson's *Strange Case of Dr Jekyll and Mr Hyde* (1886).

As you can see when comparing this topic to the essay topic previously discussed, a lot more time will be devoted to research for a term paper than an essay. The topic is no longer a vague description of a phenomenon such as 'duality', which can be interpreted in several different ways, but the concrete technical term of *doppelgänger*, which is a common motif in Gothic and horror stories. If you have not heard the term used in literary studies before, you may be surprised to find that its use is not restricted to two people who look alike, which Jekyll and Hyde, for example, do not, although Hyde is still considered the *doppelgänger* of Jekyll. Research the origins and literary history of the term. Contextualize the motif with secondary literature (you may find out that Sigmund Freud wrote about the *doppelgänger* in his essay "The Uncanny", which was, of course, published long after Steven-son's novel). Decide which aspects of the motif you are going to look at in your paper. Look for books and articles exploring the motif in Stevenson's novel, and the different ways they interpret it. Evaluate which of them will help you build and articulate your own arguments. Keep in mind that a research paper is like a miniature version of a monograph or an article in a scholarly journal, and it should be written with as much care and thought.

## Portfolio

A portfolio is a modern form of assessment, gradually begin-ning to replace research papers in some subjects, such as art or didactics. Originally, the term 'portfolio' denoted a collec-tion of financial investments (such as shares or bonds), how-ever, nowadays its meaning extends to a collection of any-thing that is considered valuable, such as an artist's portfolio of his works or the assets and qualifications a candidate pre-sents at a job interview.

Instead of writing one long document of 10-20 pages at the end of the semester or term, you will be asked to collect a variety of materials over the course of a semester. If you are in a Master of Education or teacher training programme, you may be required to submit a teaching portfolio containing lesson plans and teaching materials. A portfolio is also a pos-sible form of assessment in a lecture. Instead of having stu-dents sit an exam, they protocol all sections of the lecture and present their reflections in a portfolio.

**Collective Writing Assignments: Blogs and Wiki Articles**

With the rise of digitalized forms of teaching and learning in the classroom of the future, electronic writing assignments are more frequently required. If your course uses a CMS (Content Management System) or learning platform such as Moodle or Ilias, you may be asked to comment on an article in a seminar blog or write a wiki article for a seminar.

In a **seminar blog**, your lecturer may post articles and multimedia content. You may be asked to discuss an aspect of the post, or give feedback on additional materials. Remember that "[b]logging isn't just about writing posts; it's about sharing your learning and reflecting on what you have learnt".[4] If you write on a seminar blog, stay friendly and respectful no matter if you agree with what has been written by other people, as you would when giving feedback face-to-face in class. Do not say that you did not find an article helpful, but describe why. Remember you are not within the protected space of your seminar, you are online and visible to everyone, so never post any personal details such as your birthday or phone number.

A **wiki,** derived from the Hawaiian word for 'fast', is a web-based tool for creating and editing texts so content can quickly and easily be managed by a group of people, such as a lexicon, encyclopaedia or other type of knowledge base.[5] You have been told that you are not supposed to use Wikipedia and similar sites in your academic writing for precisely this reason – anyone can edit it. A wiki can, however, be a useful tool in courses which involve a lot of difficult terminology, for example, a wiki on terminology used in literary studies which

---

[4]  Sue Waters, "Create a Class Blog". *The EduBlogger*. Web. 22 June 2019. <https://www.theedublogger.com/week-1-create-a-class-blog/>.

[5]  Maria Karlsberger, "E-Learning. Neue Medien in der Hochschullehre". Institut für Lehr- und Lerninnovation, Universität Erlangen-Nürnberg. Workshop script, 23 November 2012, 21.

you write with your fellow students in the introductory seminar. The advantage of a wiki is that it can easily be modified – you do not have to learn a whole markup language such as HTML, but only a few commands – and that all members of the course can use it to prepare for the exam. Other than an essay or research paper, a wiki article does not require you to interpret or analyse a topic, but to gather all essential information on a topic that your readers may find useful.

Articles for the context of seminars should be limited to 4,000 characters. Each article should contain quotations and sources. The hypertext structure allows you to link your article to related articles written by your fellow students – which means that students have to read each other's contributions. Say you are asked to write a wiki article on *Strange Case of Dr Jekyll and Mr Hyde*. In your article, you mention that it was written by Robert Louis Stevenson and that it is a Victorian Gothic novel. Link your article to the articles on Stevenson's biography, on the Victorian Age, and on the definition of Gothic, all of which were written by your fellow students. This way, you can see how your topic relates to other themes discussed in the course. Visitors who read your article and are not sure what else it was they associated Stevenson's name with can simply click on the biographical link to find out that he also wrote *Treasure Island*.

## Exercises

### Exercise 6.1: Reading Responses
Write a reading response of 300-350 words on the following text. What forms of knowledge are mentioned in the text? Assess their importance.

## William Wordsworth, "Expostulation and Reply" (*Lyrical Ballads*, 1798)

"WHY, William, on that old grey stone,
Thus for the length of half a day,
Why, William, sit you thus alone,
And dream your time away?

5    "Where are your books?--that light bequeathed
To Beings else forlorn and blind!
Up! up! and drink the spirit breathed
From dead men to their kind.

"You look round on your Mother Earth,
10    As if she for no purpose bore you;
As if you were her first-born birth,
And none had lived before you!"

One morning thus, by Esthwaite lake,
When life was sweet, I knew not why,
15    To me my good friend Matthew spake,
And thus I made reply:

"The eye--it cannot choose but see;
We cannot bid the ear be still;
Our bodies feel, where'er they be,
20    Against or with our will.

"Nor less I deem that there are Powers
Which of themselves our minds impress;
That we can feed this mind of ours
In a wise passiveness.

25    "Think you, 'mid all this mighty sum
Of things for ever speaking,
That nothing of itself will come,
But we must still be seeking?

„--Then ask not wherefore, here, alone,
30    Conversing as I may,
I sit upon this old grey stone,
And dream my time away."

***Annotations:*** expostulation = an attack, a reproach; Esthwaite lake: an idyllic place in the Lake District; spake = spoke; wherefore = why

## Exercise 6.2: Different Types of Texts
What would you have to do differently if you were to write an essay or term paper?

You have found a topic, identified some sources, evaluated their content, and written an abstract for your research paper – congratulations, you are ready to start writing! Maybe you are lucky enough to write the entire paper between terms, during the holidays, and you can focus entirely on the writing process. Perhaps you have to write during the semester, or you are working, trying to find the time to write in the evenings. In any case, you will want to organize the writing process well and stick to a writing routine. Reserve some time for writing, and insist on it. Do not be persuaded by a flat-mate to do the dishes or go shopping; do not "quickly" check your e-mails or answer incoming messages on your phone before you start working. Let your flat-mates, friends, and family know that you will be working for the next couple of hours and cannot be disturbed. Software such as AntiSocial can be useful tools to prevent distractions; once activated, they block all communicative functions of the internet such as e-mail or social networks until you reboot your computer.

Time and workplace may also be decisive factors for the success of your writing project. Some students prefer working at the library, others avoid neutral environments because they require the creative chaos of their own desk. A change of scene may be required once in a while – why not work through your secondary sources at a café or in the park? Some set their alarm to five in the morning to avoid the background noise at their halls of residence, others are more productive at night. If possible, you should adapt your working conditions to your personal habits and needs. Some students start with the main body of their research paper, writing the introduction last. This way, you can summarize your findings in the conclusion and then, knowing what it is that you have found out, ask the right questions in your introduction. Theoretically – in practice, most students end up writing their conclusion in a hurry because the deadline is fast approaching, and then they remember they have not even started on their introduction. Ultimately, both the first and the final chapter tend to be badly written, ruining the overall impression of a carefully orchestrated paper. Do not fall into the trap of writing your introduction under pressure. Reserve enough time to write a strong introduction and a concise conclusion. The advantage of actually starting with the introduction is that you make up your mind about the research questions and the goals of your paper before you start writing. When your paper is finished, you can still re-read and revise your introduction. Look out for the questions asked in your introduction – have they been answered in your conclusion? Ideally, those two chapters should be to your text like a frame to a picture. You would not buy a frame for a Picasso at your local discounter, would you?

## 7.1 Table of Contents – the Skeleton of Your Paper

Think of your table of contents as the skeleton of your paper. Muscles and tendrils would not be able to move your limbs without any bones to provide structure and stability, your inner organs would not remain where they are most efficient. If you write a paper without having at least a vague idea of how you are going to structure your arguments, your text is likely to be associative, jumping from one idea to the other without a cohesive line of argument. A rough draft of your table of contents can guide you through the writing process. Remember: no one will force you to stick to it religiously if you find out that not all aspects of it were brilliant. Before the deadline, nothing is cast in stone forever. There is nothing worse than a table of contents whose central buzz words are never mentioned in the text because the writer changed his or her mind and forgot to adapt the table of contents to the new line of argument. It is nonetheless advisable to think of a rough draft of a table of contents before you start writing. It will provide a plan for the steps you are going to take, a golden thread to follow. Which terms and definitions are required? Which themes are you going to analyse? What do you hope to accomplish, what are your goals? What matters is that you ask these questions of the text or topic before you start writing; the precise phrasing can wait.

How do you go about writing an academic paper, or better yet, how should you not do it? Tongue-in-cheek, Joan Bolker, in her book *Writing Your Dissertation in 15 Minutes a Day* (1998), describes a typical writing process that has been taught to countless generations of students, but is not exactly suited to inducing enthusiasm for academic writing:

> First you choose a topic […]. Then you researched the topic (this step seemed to involve a lot of index cards). Then you thought about your topic (I've always imagined here a cartoon of someone sitting at a desk, with an empty word balloon attached to her head).
>
> Having thought, you made an outline for your paper, then wrote, starting with I,1 on your outline, fleshing it out, making sure you had a good topic sentence for each paragraph. You proceeded through the outline in order, and when you finished, and capped the paper off with a final, summarizing paragraph, you let the paper rest for a day (sort of like bread dough), then came back, checked the grammar, spelling, transitions, and diction, and cleaned all of them up. Then you were done. I don't think this model worked. Much of the time it led to neat, clean, boring papers, often to empty ones with good form.[1]

Bolker's method concentrates on first developing a personal approach to the topic. Of course, no one can write a doctoral thesis or even a research paper in 15 minutes a day; yet the thought-provoking title expresses two of the most important principles when writing a paper: firstly, dividing a large

---

[1]   Joan Bolker, *Writing Your Dissertation in Fifteen Minutes a Day* (New York: Henry and Holt, 1998), 32-3.

project into subprojects, and secondly, perseverance. The latter is more easily achieved if you are actually curious about your topic and if you enjoy creating something new. Choose a topic you are, if not passionate about, at least strongly interested in. Brainstorm about your topic, figure out an original approach, rather than merely summarizing secondary literature. When you are done with research, however, you cannot escape from doing a bit of boring structural work.

The following example illustrates how to create a Table of Contents.

### Aspects of Theodicy in John Milton's *Paradise Lost*

The term 'theodicy' is essential to the topic. This implies that your introduction will explore the meaning of this term, providing a first definition: if God is good and almighty, why is there evil in the world? As your primary text is *Paradise Lost*, use the introduction to position the term of theodicy within the context of the epic. Identify passages in the text where the question of God's justice in the face of evil is asked, explicitly or implicitly. Your body of theory will look at theodicy in more detail, adding philosophical and historical contexts. In your analysis, you will discuss the passages of the text concerned with evil and justice. In your conclusion, summarize how the problem of theodicy is handled in Milton's epic and why it is important for the plot. These reflections form the basis of your table of contents.

### Draft 1: Structure and Questions

**Introduction:** What is theodicy? Why do I look at it in Milton's *Paradise Lost?*

**Body of Theory:** What are the origins of the problem of theodicy? What are some typical stances in philosophy, theology, literature? Why would it be important during the time Milton was writing?

**Text Analysis:** How is theodicy handled in *Paradise Lost*?

**Conclusion:** Summarize, evaluate – what is the answer of the epic to the problem of theodicy, if any?

Now try to plan your line of argument in your body of theory and your text analysis. Include the secondary sources you have already consulted and your own notes on the text. Identify buzz words you are going to include later. Note that an introduction should not simply be called 'Introduction" without providing any clues regarding its content. The same is true for the conclusion.

### Draft 2: Chapters and Keywords

1. Introduction: "Si deus, unde malum?" Theodicy as Charges Against God
2. Historical Positions in the Debate on Theodicy
   2.1 Theodicy in Antiquity and Middle Ages (Epicurus, *privatio boni*)
   2.2 Leibniz and Optimism
3. Aspects of Theodicy in John Milton's *Paradise Lost*
   3.1 Theodicy as Central Aim of the Epic Voice ("But Vindicate the Ways of God to Man")
   3.2 Portrayal of Evil, Characterisation and Comments Concerning Evil
4. Conclusion: Justification of the Existence of Evil (*felix culpa* Argument)

Now you have already drafted the steps of your analysis. Insert subchapters when it is sensible to divide a chapter into several steps or discuss aspects separately. This draft forms the basis of your Table of Contents. Use nouns whenever possible. Eliminate whole sentences or questions from your final Table. Observe the rules of capitalization in English texts ("Table of Contents", not "Table of contents" or "Table Of Contents"). In English, rules of capitalization apply to titles and subtitles (not only the title of your paper, but also titles of works you list in your bibliography) as well as to headings in a Table of Contents.

Capital letters: the first word of the title, the final word, and other words carrying meaning (also the second part of a compound), for example: nouns, pronouns, verbs, adjectives, adverbs, subordinating conjunctions (after, although, as if, as soon as, because, before, if, that, unless, until, when, where, while). Small letters: articles (the, a, an), prepositions (of, in), coordinating conjunctions (and, but, for, nor, or, so, yet), 'to' in infinitives (*How to Write a Research Paper*). Note that 'as' can be used as a conjunction, preposition, or adverb, depending on the context – in *The Critic as Artist*, 'as' is a preposition and should not be capitalized.

### Draft 3: Complete Table of Contents

1. Introduction: "Si Deus, Unde Malum?" Theodicy as Charge Against God
2. Historical Positions in the Debate on Theodicy
    2.1 Theodicy in Antiquity and the Middle Ages
        2.1.1 Epicurus' Unholy God Problem and Underachiever Problem
        2.1.2 Evil as *Privatio Boni* in Patristic Philosophy
    2.2 Leibniz and Optimism
3. Aspects of Theodicy in John Milton, *Paradise Lost* (1666)
    3.1 Explicit Theodicy: Aim of the Epic Voice
    3.2 Implicit Theodicy: Evil in Paradise Lost
        3.2.1 Battle Between Good and Evil
        3.2.2 Satan as Aestheticization of Evil
        3.2.3 Unmasking Evil: Imagery
        3.2.4 Sin as "Fortunate Fall"
4. Conclusion: The *Felix Culpa* Argument as Response to Theodicy

    Bibliography

When you have finished formatting your manuscript, do not forget to add page numbers (word processing programmes generate a Table of Contents automatically). Your bibliography (like an appendix containing additional materials) will be in your Table of Contents, but not numbered. Your affidavit is attached to the paper, but not listed in the Table of Contents.

## 7.2 Introductions: "Interesting" Topic, but why?

One of the most common mistakes in term papers is the lack of an adequate introduction and a meaningful concluding part. If you anticipate all your arguments in an introduction, you are harming your work by raising expectations that cannot be met. That is why many people tend not to reveal anything in the introduction. Instead, they verbalise the structure of the paper; the Table of Contents is regurgitated and chewed again. The reader quickly feels bored or underestimated – don't you trust him to understand your Table of Contents without your assistance? It is just as wrong, however, to provide the author's biography or historical information in the introduction if these have no relevance to the topic at all. Superfluous information absorbs the attention of your reader without contributing to your arguments.

In addition, especially at the beginning of your studies, you will first have to acquire the basic historical knowledge of your discipline. As a freshman, you tend to simplify or distort facts. Finally, the worst conceivable variant of an introduction is reducing your motivation to work on this topic to a lame "it's so interesting!". If you have nothing to say about the relevance of the topic for your field, about its being unfairly underrated in studies, about the virulence of your text, or its ground-breaking significance for an entire genre, no one will believe you that the topic is really so exciting. You might as well write: "Unfortunately, I have to write this paper to complete the module".

Probably the readers of your paper will not be familiar with each and every detail of the topic you are writing about. Therefore, in the introduction, you should help them find access to your subject. If you manage to write a 'user-friendly' introduction and, at the same time, prove that you stand out from boring, uninspired introductions and know the value of your topic in a broader context, your reader is almost on your side already. Proceed according to the premise: "You never get a second chance to make a first impression".

The shape: The introduction should include at least three quarters of a page to one page for ten to twelve pages of text. Both the introduction and the conclusion must have a heading. It is up to you whether or not you write "Introduction: Changes in the Perception of Natural Knowledge in Seventeenth-Century Britain" or just "Changes in the Perception of Natural Knowledge in Seventeenth-Century Britain" – as long as you do not leave it at "Introduction".

The introduction should **guide** your reader **towards the topic**. Do not write anything that is nothing to do with your problem. **After reading your introduction, there should be no doubt in your reader's mind what the central theme of your work is.**

Put away your Table of Contents when writing your introduction. That way you will not be tempted to just verbalize what you are planning to discuss in each chapter. Relate a historical event, discuss a contextualized quotation from primary or secondary literature (provocative quotations are particularly suitable here), or address a central concept of your topic directly, leading to the questions you intend to answer. Find out about the current state of research on your topic. The argument "for a better understanding of the text you have to take a closer look at xy" does not apply – what exactly do you want to illustrate about the text, why? Define key terms, or at least raise the definitory problem that you will address in the theoretical part. Use reported or indirect questions instead of direct ones for a more academic and formal style.

There are different approaches to beginning an academic text, as the following examples illustrate.

### 1) Starting from a suitable quotation

Find a memorable quote from literature that is characteristic of the issues you want to address in your paper.

> "Justice was done, and the President of the Immortals, in the Aeschylan phrase, had ended his sport with Tess" (Hardy 489)

> With these words Thomas Hardy's novel Tess of the d'Urbervilles ends. God's apparently injust action, which plunges the innocent protagonist into misery for no reason, cannot be reconciled with the Christian notion of an omnipotent and beneficient God. God seems rather to resemble the immortals of Greek tragedy, whose actions are often marked by vindictiveness, arbitrariness, and sadism. Hardy's pessimistic phrase represents a paradox that has preoccupied theology since its earliest origins: theodicy.

### 2) Starting from the historical context

Place your topic in a historical or theoretical context. What developments have led to the specific characteristics of your theme? How does your text affect other texts from the same period or later periods?

> The notion of traveling as a form of education has been established in English travel literature by the eighteenth century. The traveling subject undergoes significant changes while experiencing the other, as was the purpose of the classical *Grand Tour.* The end of the journey also marks a new stage of development in the personal history of the narrator. Exposing oneself to the other and mastering the difficulties traveling entails is thus understood as a method of self-improvement. Chloe Chard terms this perspective on traveling the 'Romantic Approach': '"travel is a form of personal adventure, holding out the promise of a discovery or realization of the self through the exploration of the 'Other'" (Chard 11).

Be sure to avoid unacceptable generalizations in this approach, such as: "The prudery of the Victorians..", "The Modernists were pessimistic…"

### 3) Starting from a historical anecdote

Anecdotes are entertaining case studies well suited to presenting complex facts in a simplified form. Since you will discuss the topic in its entire complexity in the main part, you can use an anecdote as an introduction to a larger context. Please note that it must be a historical anecdote – not based on your personal experience in primary school!

> In April 1929, Albert Einstein received a telegram from the New York rabbi Herbert Goldstein. The Rabbi had been startled because a Boston Cardinal had warned his congregation not to study relativity, claiming that it tried to pass off atheistic ideas to an unsuspecting audience. Goldstein's telegram read: "Do you believe in God? STOP. Paid answer: 50 words". Einstein's theory of relativity represented a caesura in the Christian world view, which called the absolutes of space and time into question. The loss of fixed reference systems, challenging what people thought they knew for a fact, led to a great uncertainty, especially regarding faith and religion…

### 4) Starting from the current state of research

Such an approach requires a detailed examination of the current sources on your topic. You can also combine this approach with a quotation, as the following introduction from a student paper demonstrates using the contrasting terms *luminous historians* and *prostitute writers*:

> The term 'luminous historian' was coined by Patricia Craddock, who uses the term for the title of her book on […] Edward Gibbon, one of the greatest historians of the Enlightenment (Craddock *n.pag.*). Concerning oneself with historiography in the period that is often referred to as the Age of Enlightenment, one is confronted with a type of neoclassical historiography that in its perception, in many aspects, differs from that of modern historiography. Thus in the eighteenth century historians such as Voltaire saw in the study of history, especially ancient

history, the possibility of discovering universal truths about human nature and civil society (Bourgault and Sparling 5). […] It shall be essential
to trace the change of perception of history writing, especially when
contrasting neoclassical historiography with a type of literary criticism,
which was proposed by writers such as Stephen Greenblatt and Hayden
White, beginning in the late 1970s, and the New Historicism.

A central aspect of this approach is the idea that the relationship between literature and history is reciprocal. History-
writing in general is often subjected to critique, especially,
because the ones writing about history are often considered
to be biased. At the same time they are being criticised for
not being able to give an accurate representation of historical
facts without – intentionally or not – manipulating the history, which is narrated to achieve a certain goal.

This case study is going to concern itself with […] historiography, [in]
the Glubbdubdrib episode of *Gulliver's Travels*, focusing on the role of
historians whom Swift depicts as 'prostitute writers'. To [illumine …]
the theoretical background of Swift's criticism of historians, [reference
will be made to the] so called *Querelle des Anciens et des Modernes*,
which will identify Swift as a prominent figure of this controversy. The
character of Gulliver himself can be seen as a sort of historian and
therefore is subject to his own criticism; this constitutes a first step to
conclude on the central question of this paper, whether history is ultimately nothing but storytelling.[2]

### 5) Starting from central terms.
In a paper on the historical novel in England and its development towards historiographical metafiction, it is advisable to
clearly define terms such as "historical" and "historical novel"
in the introduction. Detailed discussions can then be followed
by a theoretical part.

---

[2]   Franziska Aurnhammer, "History and Storytelling in the Eighteenth Century
with Regard to *Gulliver's Travels*: 'Luminous Historians' or 'Prostitute Writers'?" Unpublished term paper, seminar "Knowledge in Eighteenth-Century
Literature", WS 2014/15, FAU Erlangen-Nürnberg. Reproduced with kind
permission of the author.

Georg Lukác's influential monograph *The Historical Novel,* first published in German as *Der historische Roman,*[3] marks the beginning of the historical novel at the beginning of the 19th century in close connection with the person of Sir Walter Scott. Although Lukács admits that literary genres that claim to be historical have already emerged, they are "historical only in theme and costume".[4] With these, the events of the novel itself are transported into the past, but the psychology and behaviour of the characters are taken directly from the present of their authors.[5]

## 6) "Inverted Pyramid Method"

The origins of the inverted pyramid method lie in journalism. The method describes the procedure of placing the "base" of the pyramid, *i.e.* the most important facts (in journalistic texts the so-called W-questions), at the beginning of the article.[6] When writing for blogs, websites or text messages in the newspaper, it is practical to start with the most important aspect in order to quickly provide readers with the salient bits of information. In academia, the metaphor is adapted:

Every time you begin a new subject, think of an inverted pyramid – The broadest range of information sits at the top, and as the paragraph or paper progresses, the author becomes more and more focused on the argument ending with specific, detailed evidence supporting a claim. Lastly, the author explains how and why the information she has just

---

[3]    Georg Lukács, *Der historische Roman. Probleme des Realismus III*, Band 6 (Neuwied und Berlin: Luchterhand, 1965 [1936]).

[4]    Georg Lukács, *The Historical Novel*, trans. Hannah and Stanley Mitchell (Lincoln: University of Nebraska Press, 1983), 34.

[5]    See Simone Broders, *"As if a building was being constructed" – Studien zur Rolle der Geschichte in den Romanen Adam Thorpes. Reihe: Erlanger Studien zur Anglistik und Amerikanistik*, Bd. 10 (Münster: LIT, 2008), 12-3.

[6]    "The inverted pyramid puts the most newsworthy information at the top, and then the remaining information follows in order of importance, with the least important at the bottom". Chip Scanlan,"Writing from the Top Down: Pros and Cons of the Inverted Pyramid". Poynter Institute. Web. 20 April 2015. <http://www.poynter.org/news/media-innovation/12754/writing-from-the-top-down-pros-and-cons-of-the-inverted-pyramid/>.

provided connects to and supports her thesis (a brief wrap up or warrant).[7]

Start with a broad base of general information and backgrounds on the topic and move **from general to specific**. At the end there is the delimitation of the topic question (in reported speech).

### Inverted Pyramid – From General to Specific

Broad base of general information,
Backgrounds on the topic

Specifics on the topic

Central
aspect

### Example: (excerpt)

**Topic: Sir Francis Bacon – the 'Father' of Empiricism? Observations on Selected Texts**

Before the Age of Enlightenment had started to gradually arise in Britain from the middle of the 17th century [...], philosophers were still convinced of the theoretical correctness and accuracy of the ancient Greek philosopy of Aristotle and his conclusion that if sufficiently clever men only discussed a topic for long enough, the desirable 'truth' about nature would eventually be discovered. [...]

Then, beginning in the 1650s, local thinkers in urban coffeehouses or salons, commonly called 'natural philosophers', began to meet in London to debate new scientific ideas and inventions [...], promoting knowledge of the natural world not only through discussion, but by observation and the conduction of experiments [.].

Yet the question of who or what exactly had influenced and ignited the change in people's ways of thinking about how to approximate

---

[7]    "Body paragraphs: Moving from general to specific information". Purdue Writing Lab. Web. 20 September 2019. < https://owl.purdue.edu/owl/general_writing/common_writing_assignments/argument_papers/body_paragraphs.html>.

nature – now taking an empiricist approach – is still a matter discussed within the current scientific community. [...]

   "Knowledge is Power" is the motto of a man who was not only an English statesman but also an essayist, historian, philosopher, and scientist – Sir Francis Bacon. His works, especially the *Advancement of Learning*, in which he proposed an entirely new system based on empirical and inductive principles and which ultimately, the goal was the production of practical knowledge for the use and benefit of man (Simpson *n.pag.*) was not received with much attention at the time he lived (1561-1626), yet afterwards.[8]

This introduction begins with a general presentation of knowledge in the Western philosophical tradition and then moves on to the more specific details, empiricism and the role of Sir Francis Bacon in its emergence in Britain.

   Do not give the reader overly detailed information (save those for the main part) yet, but specify **which terms and definitions** are important for your work. Draw attention to the **central problem** of your paper, the topic. In your final section, you will refer back to the questions that have arisen here. Your central theme should be the culmination of your introduction, not just repeated in slightly different words to fill a page. Why is your question relevant? How does an investigation of this question help to understand the whole text? (avoid phrases such as "it is interesting" – they are not very meaningful).

   **Avoid meta-text**, which is basically pure verbalization of your Table of Contents ("It is the purpose of this paper to... In the first chapter, an overview will be given of... In the second chapter, an analysis of xyz will be provided..."). In a good term paper, the structure can be concluded from the text. **Take full advantage of** the introduction instead – now you have the full attention of your readers, keep it! Clarify what

---

8    Lisa Dupont, "Sir Francis Bacon – the 'Father' of Empiricism? Observations on Selected Texts". Unpublished paper in the proseminar "Knowledge in Eighteenth-Century British Literature", WS 2014/15, FAU Erlangen-Nürnberg. Reproduced (slightly abbreviated) with kind permission of the author.

your work is about, why your topic is so relevant, which problems are related to your topic. Promote your topic! Give your readers the feeling that they will not waste their time with your paper.

## 7.3 Convincing Arguments

When the first hurdle of the introduction has been cleared, the real work begins: building your arguments. Many students believe that they only have to create a collage of quotations in the analytical part of their work. This assumption is fundamentally wrong. Other people's ideas are intended to give you an overview to help you form a well-founded academic opinion. The criteria that make up a very good academic piece of work will differ individually, depending on the student's qualifications, or subject matter, and the lecturer's priorities. In general, however, it can be said that most lecturers look for the following aspects:

- **Dealing with academic text.** Is the topic sufficiently covered by literature? As already described in the section on secondary literature, it does not always have to be "interpretations". Theoretical backgrounds, contexts, or reviews are at least as important as text analysis. The range of sources is also a criterion. If you have only worked with the first few hits on your favourite search engine, this does not prove that you are able to order a book via interlibrary loan or to obtain an essay that you have found in a database. It is equally important that the sources you use are as up-to-date as possible. A book from the 1950s will tell you nothing about the current state of research, many statements are certainly already outdated. In addition, you have to show that you can quote and paraphrase correctly.

- **Methodological considerations.** Are you aware of the scope of the problem? Can you narrow down what else belongs to your topic and what does not? Think about a suitable approach. Do you first work out a theoretical part and then apply the theory to the text? Do you first treat two texts separately in order to create a comparison in the third part? Do you write from a feminist, psychological, poststructuralist, or neo-historical perspective, and why is this approach particularly suitable for your topic? In addition to choosing the right approach, focusing on the topic is also a methodological consideration. Is the "golden thread" recognizable in your work? Has it become clear what your research question is and how you intend to solve it?
- **Presentation.** Is your submitted manuscript visually appealing? Does it adhere to style specifications (*e.g.* style sheets of your institute, *MLA Handbook*)? Has your paper been proofread with regard to typos, grammar, and spelling? Do you adhere to a matter-of-fact, sober style? Do you master your word processing programme (spacing, indents)?
- **Analysis and interpretation**. Is your topic sufficiently covered by your analysis? Is your argumentation conclusive, or are there logical breaks? Do you know your primary text well and use it competently to support your reasoning? How well do you handle secondary literature? Can you cite and paraphrase accurately? Can you critically weigh up whether the arguments of others are conclusive, and are you credible in your position? Can you weigh up different arguments that contradict each other and can you assess their strengths and weaknesses? Have you come to useful conclusions, have you drawn conclusions from the interpretation? Have you expressed yourself well, is your wording clear and concise?

Show that you have carefully read and understood the material. The best way to do this is to explain and interpret what information you have extracted from your sources and how these statements should be evaluated. Think critically and look at a problem from all sides, instead of making sweeping judgments, or adopting the statements of others without reflection. You should have a clear stance and try to convince the reader of your arguments. Therefore, all chains of evidence that you set up must be complete and logical in themselves. Relate your own argumentation to the arguments you have read in secondary literature, which cannot replace your own work, only supplement it. Do not leave quotations uncommented, even if you share the author's opinion. The further you progress in your studies, the more autonomy you will have to demonstrate.

**Example: Building Your Own Arguments**
**Critical evaluation of Secondary Literature, Topic: Cultural Studies, Function of Shakespeare Quotes in Gene Roddenberry's *Star Trek***
Have a look at the secondary source which is going to be used in building the argument:

> An example of [...] repressive use of Shakespeare may be found in "The Perfect Mate", an episode of *The Next Generation* first broadcast in April 1992. "The Perfect Mate" concerns the effects of male heterosexual desire on Captain Picard and his crew. As this essay will show, the episode is misogynistic and homophobic and underwrites its ideology with the motif of Shakespeare's sonnets – the quintessential symbol of love poetry in our culture. [...] The objectification of Kamala as essentialized, idealized woman is continued in her objectified status as a gift/slave. [...] Kamala remains nothing more than an object of exchange, the figure of threatening and alluring woman. [..] *Star Trek: The Next Generation* consistently destabilizes its progressive ethos with sexism [...]. There are better uses for Shakespeare than lending cultural authority to oppressive gender stereotypes. Those have too much authority in our culture already.[9]

---

[9]    Emily Hegarty, "Some Suspect of Ill: Shakespeare's *Sonnets* and 'The Perfect Mate'". *Extrapolation*, 36/1, 1995; 55-64; 56, 58, 63.

The central **thesis** of the extract is:

*Star Trek: The Next Generation* uses motifs from Shakespeare's sonnets to oppress women.

**Argument:**

The episode "The Perfect Mate" is a misogynistic episode in which Shakespeare's sonnets are used to install the main character Kamala, a kind of "dark lady" who is forcibly married in peace negotiations, as the prototype of the *femme fatale*. Kamala is no more than a slave of the patriarchal system. Moreover, the episode is homophobic, since no "Fair Youth" is established alongside the "Dark Lady" (**examples** from the episode and from Shakespeare's sonnets follow, not quoted here).

**Conclusions:**

Shakespeare is abused in *Star Trek* as a cultural justification for patriarchal authority. By subscribing to this form of sexism, *Star Trek* destroys the *per se* progressive concept of the *franchise*.

In one' s own academic work it is now necessary to critically examine the statements of secondary literature. Ask yourself the following questions:

- Does the reasoning apply to this particular episode?
- Does the reasoning apply to the overall context of the series or franchise? Are there other examples or counter-examples in other episodes?
- What other factors should be considered, *e.g.* cultural and historical contexts in the year of origin?

Go through the author's reasoning in detail. Consult more secondary literature if you feel you lack the expertise.

Use the example to research political and social events of the production year in order to identify possible allusions to current events.

**Possible Solutions:**

- **Context of quotations.** Kamala talks about the "Dark Lady" only in one scene of the episode: When she discovers a Shakespeare edition in the captain's ready room, she immediately falls back on the role she is supposed to play of empathizing with the men around her; "because one never knows when a conversation might turn to [..] the dark woman of raven brows and mournful eyes of Shakespeare's s sonnets" (23:25). Only later does she have the opportunity to reflect on Picard's critical questions about what she herself expects from her life and makes her own decisions.

- **Context within the episode.** The series positions itself also within the episode against the reduction of Kamala to an object; the ship's female chief medical officer Crusher even speaks of "prostitution". Besides, the use of the sonnet could also represent the idea of *unrequited love*.

- **Context of the series and the *Star Trek* franchise.** *The Next Generation* sets itself apart from the marginalization of women (original series from the 1960s): the same uniforms for male and female officers, women in leadership positions, and, in the Spin-Offs *Star Trek: Voyager* and *Discovery,* a woman in the leading role. The theme of arranged marriage was already taken up in the episode "Haven" and treated very critically. Homosexuality was negotiated in detail in the episode "The Outcast", and the spin-off *Star Trek: Deep Space Nine* showed one of the first homosexual couples in a US TV series. In *Discovery*, a homosexual couple was established in the cast permanently. There is no evidence that the omission of "Fair Youth" in the constellation of persons was done with the intention to exclude homosexual relationships from the franchise.

- **Context of the production year 1992:** There were several divorces in the British Royal family, the episode might

be an allusion to those events and as such a plea for free-
dom of choice.[10]

Now contextualize your own argumentation with the secondary literature. It is important that you do not "tear the secondary literature to pieces" or ridicule it. Deal objectively with the
arguments, but also clarify your own academic point of view.

Always be critical of secondary literature. The mere fact that
a thesis has been printed does not mean that it is correct.
Conversely, of course, you should not criticize just for the sake
of criticism. Show that you can develop a well-founded academic point of view.

**Work discursively** – each topic has more than one side, so
you should also present these different aspects. For example,
the period of modernity (from around 1910) can be understood
as a period of new beginnings, but at the same time there are
many arguments for seeing it as the period of an ending or
transition. Consider different perspectives in your work.

Your statements should remain clear and binding. Constant
hedging such as "it seems as if", "probably", "possibly" weak-
en your line of argument as a whole.


## 7.4 Conclusions in Which Something Is Concluded

In your introduction, you outlined the problem of your paper
and asked key questions, which you should work on in the
argumentative part. In the final part, you draw a conclusion
and should ideally have found a solution for all questions
raised in the introduction. Summarize your arguments and
results for the reader; this will illustrate how you proceeded

---

[10]    The critical discussion of Shakespeare in *Star Trek* was adapted from the following paper: Simone Broders, "'TaH pagh, taHbe'' – Shakespearean Heritage in
the Postmodern Space Opera". Shakespeare 450 Anniversary Conference. Par-
is, Sorbonne, 21-27 April 2014. *Cf.* <http://shakespeare.revues.org/?lang=en>

and what your results are. Having spend weeks dealing with the topic, it is completely obvious to you which conclusion has resulted from which steps of your analysis; nevertheless, you should take the trouble to summarise the salient aspects once again for your readers; this demonstrates that you have retained an eye for the essentials despite all the complexity, and that you have solved a complex and demanding task.

> *Hodd*, like *Vanity Fair*, is after all a "novel without heroes". The aging monk Much is not a character with potential for immersion or identification. Although he claims to repent of his sins, he is more distressed by the fact that he has committed a forgery of history by singing hymns of praise to Robert Hodd than by the death of two people for which he is responsible. Even the hermit seems less heroic. Much's original reason for leaving was that he let a shipwrecked sailor drown because he had not yet finished saying his morning prayers. Robert Hodd believes himself to be a demigod, determined to bring about the end of the world, terrorizing the people around him.
>
> The characters of the medieval world are bound to remain alien to the recipients of the present, a feeling that connects them with the translator Francis Belloes. The figure of Francis Belloes seems to offer a starting point for familiarity, but his story remains incomplete. Like his research object Robin Hood, Francis Belloes has disappeared into the darkness of history after only a few decades. Despite all his efforts, the past remains a 'foreign country" to the historian, a territory that keeps eluding him.[11]

Reserve the final part for the renewed, precise presentation of your most important statements – new arguments are just as out of place in the final part as detailed information. Limit the conclusion to general statements on your topic that you have already substantiated and present their relevance. It is also a good idea to give an outlook.

Therefore, do not simply stop writing, but find a concluding sentence that ideally serves as a bridge to your introduction.

---

[11]  Simone Broders, "'Feigning turned into diabolical untruth'? – Robin Hood and the mnemonic turn". 9th Erlangen Graduate Conference: Critical Perspectives: 'Turns', Trends und Theorien. 20-22 November 2009, Friedrich-Alexander-Universität Erlangen-Nürnberg.

Avoid clichéd, platitudinous final sentences ("That is why this topic is still so important today", "That is how the drama illustrates its socio-political criticism", "Thus it can easily be seen why the novel is still so popular"). You sound as if you do not feel like writing anymore.

## 7.5 Language and Style

While most students spend a lot of time on the content of their papers, formal and stylistic aspects are sometimes neglected. It is only the content that matters? People will see what you mean anyway, no matter how you say it?

> When Bud, an American boy, came to school, the games master asked Alec to explain the rules of cricket to him. "Well," said Alec, "there are two sides, one out in the field and one in the pavilion. Each man in the side that's in goes out and when he's out he comes in and the next man goes in until he's out. When they're all out, the side that's been out comes in and the side that's been in goes out and tries to get the players coming in, out. When both sides have been in and out, including the not-outs, that's the end of the game."
>     "Thanks", said Bud. "I'll stick to baseball."[12]

Although the statements are certainly all correct, it is next to impossible for a non-expert to grasp the essential information, even if the text is in writing and relatively short compared to a term paper. Linguistic expression is not like a cold you can "catch" anywhere, whether you want it or not, but it helps to read many academic texts to learn the ropes. Just like cricket has its own jargon that should be mastered in order to understand the rules of the game, there are also conventions of language in the academic community.

Therefore, use a neutral, objective writing style. Colloquial expressions, personal experiences, or subjective impressions

---

[12]    Angelika Feilhauer, Cornell Ehrhardt (eds.), *Englisch lernen mit neuen Witzen* (Ravensburg: Ravensburger Buchverlag, [8]1989), 11.

that cannot be substantiated have no place in a term paper. Special attention should be paid to parts of speech, sentence structure, and the correct prepositions, especially if you are not a native speaker of English.

- Academic style. Avoid the first person pronouns in singular and plural (not "I am going to consider", "we learn that..", but: "It has to be taken into consideration…", "the narrator reveals that..").
- "On the one hand" must be followed by "on the other hand".
- Use a dictionary when in doubt. Books such as the *Longman Language Activator* will help you develop your vocabulary, Michael Swan's *Practical English Usage* will clarify grammatical problems.
- Gender-fair language: to reduce every-day sexism in society, academic texts today aim at neutralizing stereotypes in language. Write, for example, "chairperson" instead of "chairman", write sentences without generic masculine pronouns ('he' for both men and women).

Avoid typos and orthographic mistakes by asking someone else to proof-read your paper before you submit it. Word processing programmes usually have a spell-checker, however, not all mistakes can be identified by the algorithms. Please observe that proof-reading is the only acceptable help another person may provide.

## 7.6 Research Papers in Linguistics

For linguistic term papers, the same rules in terms of academic register, structure, and style apply as to cultural and literary studies. Although the conventions differ between the disciplines of English and American Studies, linguistics and literature/culture, the sense and purpose as well as the skills that you should demonstrate in your paper are the same.

It is particularly important for linguistic term papers to state the purpose of your work in the introduction as succinctly as possible in one sentence, as is usual in abstracts on linguistic essays in specialist journals.[13] The aims of your work, your approach to your topic, and the content of your hypotheses should already be revealed to the reader in the introduction:

> The main point here is that your paper is not a mystery novel; there should be no 'big reveal' at the end. Rather, you want to set up the reader's expectations so that they know up front what you're trying to argue and, while reading your paper, will see if they're convinced by how you make your arguments.[14]

Just as in a literary/cultural studies paper, the main part frequently begins with a theoretical context and the current state of research on central concepts of the subject, and the interpretation of data and facts comprises the second half of the main part. The linguistic paper also begins with laying the theoretical and descriptive groundwork for the discussion of a linguistic problem. Joanna Blaszczak describes research papers in linguistics as follows:

> As a rule, it is advisable to first describe the linguistic phenomenon on which the question is based and – if available – to present existing analyses or hypotheses about this linguistic phenomenon. [..] After you have laid the foundations for your discussion in the first half of the main part, you can now build on them and develop a discussion of the central question. [..] The texts you use should never be introduced with

---

[13]   *Cf.* Joanna Blaszczak, "Leitfaden zur Erstellung einer schriftlichen Arbeit im Fach Linguistik". Universität Potsdam, Department für Linguistik. Web. 17 April 2013. <http://www.ling.uni-potsdam.de/~kuegler/docs/wLeitfaden_Essay2.pdf>.

[14]   Lauren Hall-Lew, "How to Write an Essay in Linguistics". *Linguistics Network.* Web. 20 September 2019. <http://www.linguisticsnetwork.com/wp-content/uploads/How-to-Write-an-Essay-in-Linguistics.compressed.pdf>.

> all the aspects discussed in them [..]; only what is relevant for answering the question posed should be extracted from the texts.[15]

As in literary and cultural studies, academic literature should not be used in linguistics to replace one's own argumentation, but rather to build one's own arguments on already existing research results, to provide you with a starting point for your own results.

In contrast to literary studies, you will not interpret a primary text, but draw conclusions from a database that may have emerged from a concrete experiment. This database is your object material, for example: questionnaires, voice recordings, transcripts, corpora, or printed texts.[16]

Formally, linguistic papers are distinguished from those in literary or cultural studies by always quoting the source material directly in the text. Footnotes are only used for genuine annotations.

## 7.7 Twelve Common Errors in Research Papers: How to Dig Your Own Grave

The best way to learn how to avoid errors in research papers is to look at texts. All of the following examples are entirely fictitious, however, they problematize actual errors occurring each semester. Read the texts closely. Reflect on what you like, and what could be improved. What would you write the same way, what would you do differently? Read the text through the eyes of your lecturer. Are there any glaring errors

---

[15]   Blaszczak, n.pag.

[16]   On the special requirements for linguistic term papers and practical examples from linguistics *cf*. Karsten Schmidtke-Bode, "Practical Guidelines for Writing a Paper in Linguistics". Friedrich-Schiller-Universität Jena. Department of English and American Studies. English Linguistics: Language and Cognition. Web. 17 September 2019.
<http://www.kschmidtkebode.de/PracticalGuidelinesforPapersinLinguistics.pdf>

you can identify right away? Take notes of everything that strikes you. Then check the commentary below.

## Example #1: Table of Contents, Topic: "Analysis of the Female Characters Rebecca and Rowena in Sir Walter Scotts *Ivanhoe*", 2nd Year of Study

## Example #2: From the Analytical Part, "Functions of the Supernatural in Ann Radcliffe's *A Sicilian Romance*"

The supernatural occurs in Ann Radcliffe's *A Sicilian Romance* several times, especially in Chapter 6, when Ferdinand is held captive. In the dungeon, he hears strange noises such as sighs, and is convinced that it must be the spirit of della Campos. He persuades Peter, who is guarding him, to watch with him in the cell during the night. As he does not want to harm an innocent man, Ferdinand refuses to try and overwhelm Peter to break out of prison. When Peter hears the ghostly moaning again, he flees in panic and leaves Ferdinand alone in his cell. He leaves the door open, but it snaps shut. When Peter wants to check on the prisoner the next morning and hears someone in the cell, he flees for fear of the ghost. Mazzini is angry at his superstitious servant and wants to see the prisoner himself to prove that nothing supernatural is going on. Ferdinand is still in his cell and claims not to have noticed anything unusual. Mazzini makes sure that Ferdinand has not let Peter in on the secret and places Ferdinand under arrest in his room.

## Example #3: From the Introduction: "Studies on the Function of the Sublime in Ann Radcliffe's *The Mysteries of Udolpho*"

In the following chapters I would like to discuss the notion of the sublime in Ann Radcliffe's Gothic novel *The Mysteries of Udolpho* and compare the text with Edmund Burke's theoretical concept of the sublime in *A Philosophical Inquiry Into the Origins of Our Ideas of the Sublime and Beautiful*. [..] To illustrate the difference between Burke's and Radcliffe's interpretations of the sublime, I will briefly discuss Burke's theory before proceeding to Radcliffe's novel. A detailed analysis of Radcliffe's aesthetic program would go beyond the scope of this paper. Nor is it possible to describe the role of landscape depictions in the context of the novel of terror and Radcliffe's literary and socio-political stance in her early writings. The author is aware of these omissions.

## Example #4: Paragraph Introductions, Several Topics

The literary period of the Augustan Age comprises a variety of genres. William Shakespeare is one of the most famous and successful Renaissance playwrights.

Times have changed considerably: nowadays, women are financially independent from their husbands, have the right to vote and to pursue their own careers. Therefore, it is all the more interesting to take a look at the role of marriage in the sixteenth century.

## Example #5: From the Analytical Part – Studies on Jane Austen's Novels

Fitzwilliam Darcy, the main character of Jane Austen's *Pride and Prejudice*, is portrayed by Oscar winner Colin Firth in the 1995 BBC adaptation. In my opinion, he is the perfect match for the role.

In Jane Austen's *Sense and Sensibility*, the character of Marianne is selfish and naive, as she actually believes that Willoughby will marry her, although Colonel Brandon is clearly the more desirable bachelor.

## Example #6: From the Analytical Part – John Milton's *Paradise Lost*

After the Fall of Man, Adam is portrayed as belonging to the world entirely, not to Paradise any more. According to C.S. Lewis (1924), he compliments Eve on her taste, declaring that Paradise had one decisive flaw; there were not enough forbidden trees. Thus Adam and Eve lay the groundwork for all bad writers who use too many epigrammes: "The father of all the bright epigrammatic wasters and the mother of all the corrupting female novelists are now both before us".[17]

## Example #7: From the Analytical Part – Diverse Topics

Lizzy and Jane are hot chicks.
At the end of the day, Satan's just fed up with God, the Son, the angels, *etc.*

## Example #8: From the Body of Theory – "Satire in Jonathan Swift's *Gulliver's Travels*"

You cannot define precisely what satire really is. The lexicographer and essayist Samuel Johnson defined satire as "a poem in which wickedness or folly is censured".[18]

## Example #9: From the Analytical Part – Mary Wollstonecraft's Feminism

Mary Wollstonecraft faced a fundamental problem in writing her *Vindication of the Rights of Woman*: language. In the eighteenth century, there was no genuine female language to express women's concerns in their very own language, linked to female sexuality. Therefore, Wollstonecraft had to argue in terms of male logic, using marginalizing language and vocabulary.

## Example #10: From the Analytical Part – "The Role of Landscape in Mary Shelley's *Frankenstein*"

The reason for the fact that Mary Shelley has her protagonist Frankenstein pursue the Creature to the North Pole may be her passion for travelling and hiking. You can find artistic descriptions of mountainous landscapes and the frigid zones throughout the novel. These passages are, however, not too elaborate and do not stall the progress of the plot. The descriptions of landscapes were added for art's sake and were intended as embellishments.

---

[17]   C.S. Lewis, "The Fall". From *A Preface to Paradise Lost* (London and New York: Oxford UP, 1942). John Milton, *Paradise Lost*. Ed. Gordon Teskey. A Norton Critical Edition (New York: Norton, 2005), 453-55, 455.

[18]   "Satire". *Encyclopaedia Britannica Online*. Web. 28 Sept. 2019.
< https://www.britannica.com/art/satire >.

## Example #11: From the Analytical Part – "The Character of the Scientist in Mary Shelley's *Frankenstein*"

Mary Shelley's novel *Frankenstein* criticizes the dishonesty and the *hubris* of the scientist. If Victor Frankenstein had immediately confessed his creation to his friend Henry Clerval, they could have pursued the Creature together. They might even have prevented the Creature's revenge and integrated it into society, which would have added a completely new twist to the plot.

## Example #12: Trauma in D.H. Lawrence's Short Stories

In his short story "The Shadow in the Rose Garden", D.H. Lawrence treats the failure of human relationships of soldiers who attempt to recover from the trauma of World War I.

### Assessment of the Examples

### Error #1: Losing Track of the Topic

The topic of the first example is to analyse Rebecca und Rowena in Sir Walter Scotts *Ivanhoe*. The discussion of these characters does not start until page 10. Given that a research paper should comprise ten to twelve pages for a seminar in your second year of study, that is way too late. Biographical information is, in most cases, irrelevant for the term paper, unless you are writing about an autobiography; even then, an isolated chapter on the life and works of the author is not advisable, as you are expected to relate the biography to the text and elucidate its function, problematizing biographical fallacy. In our example, Sir Walter Scott's life seems unrelated to the topic. The same is true for the chapter on genre. If you wrote about historical characters and events figuring in *Ivanhoe*, discussing Scott's concept of the historical novel would be justified. In this case, it does not contribute to a better understanding of Rebecca and Rowena.

One of the reasons why authors do not even realize they are losing track of the topic is the meaningless headlines. If the introduction had a real headline containing information about what the paper is going to accomplish, the irrelevance of the subsequent summary of biographical and genre description would be evident. Using only the names of the characters as headlines does not provide any information about the content of the chapter. Your supervisor starts to wonder if there is any content at all if even you, the author, are unable to summarize it in your headline. Create meaningful headlines which hint at your findings: "Rowena as Prototype of the Conservative Ideal of Womanhood", "Rebecca – the Clandestine Heroine?". Note that the Table of Contents is lacking an essential part: an additional chapter in which the characters are compared and related to Ivanhoe.

Have you spotted the formal errors as well? The bibliography should not be numbered, and the affidavit, which is a legal requirement, but not officially part of your paper, should not be listed in the Table of Contents at all.

### Error #2: Page-Long Plot Summaries

Essentially, this text is a plot summary. Unless your lecturer has specifically asked for a summary (as might be the case with very complex or obscure texts in a dissertation), you can assume the members of your imaginary peer-group have read the primary texts. Summaries do not add to your arguments, they are regarded as a desperate attempt to fill the pages of your research paper. When referring to specific scenes or chapters, refer to the primary text only (with quotations and page numbers) – do not quote summaries of the text from secondary sources. Focus on concise statements, providing evidence from primary and secondary sources.

### Error #3: Meta-Text

In the following chapters I would like to discuss…
To illustrate the difference … I will briefly … before proceeding to Radcliffe's novel. A detailed analysis of … would go beyond the scope

> of this paper. Nor is it possible to describe.. The author is aware of
> these omissions.

Meta-text means commenting on the writing process.[19] Avoid writing about how you structure your paper, this should be clear from your Table of Contents and from the coherence of the text itself. Use sentence connectors for focusing, sequencing, linking, and drawing conclusions. Your chapters should not end abruptly, but with a miniature summary or conclusion, leading elegantly to the problems discussed in the following chapter. Instead of telling your readers how you write, use your introduction more cleverly to inform them about the focus of your paper. A lot of meta-text sounds artificial. Furthermore, meta-descriptions will distract readers from your arguments, which is actually the part of your paper you want to showcase.

"It would go beyond the scope of this paper…". Believe it or not: your lecturer knows that you are working on a 10-page paper in an introductory seminar, not on your doctoral dissertation. If topics are relatively open, it is to enable you to focus on those aspects that interest you. You do not have to show the topic in all its complexity, so stop apologizing for not writing your *opus magnum*!

### Error #4: Commonplaces and Empty Phrases

> The literary period of the Augustan Age comprises a variety of genres.

Of course, it is not wrong to note that the Augustan Age comprises a variety of genres – unfortunately, the same can be said about any literary period, not just the eighteenth century. For your topic, such an observation is irrelevant.

> William Shakespeare is one of the most famous and successful Renaissance playwrights.

---

[19]   Gérard Genette, *Palimpseste. Die Literatur auf zweiter Stufe* (Frankfurt/M: Suhrkamp, 1993), 13.

This is a fact your readers are well acquainted with. This sentence is boring and devoid of meaning. Guide your readers directly to the topic: William Shakespeare's *Macbeth*, written in 1606, shows many characteristics of Shakespeare's character tragedies: …

> Times have changed considerably: nowadays, women are financially independent from their husbands, have the right to vote and to pursue their own careers. Therefore, it is all the more interesting to take a look at the role of marriage in the sixteenth century.

This is an extremely artificial introduction to the topic. It is interesting to look at the 16th century because the situation of women has improved since then? Why the 16th century, not the Middle Ages, or the Enlightenment? Interesting for whom, and why? What is the academic relevance of such a comparison, what does the research question consist in? For each and every sentence you write, consider if it contributes to your argument. If that is not the case, forget about it. Stop telling your readers why your topic is 'interesting'. Of course it can be very rewarding if you enjoy doing research about your topic, but your interest is not a convincing argument for your readers. Tell them why they should pay attention to your work, why your topic is relevant for the field.

### Error #5: Subjective Opions
It goes without saying that you are entitled to your own opinion – remember though that you are supposed to write an academic paper, not a personal essay or a review of the book or film. Awards of individual actors obviously does not illustrate your point either.

Feel free to draw conclusions, but do so on the basis of your research and a logical line of argument, not your subjective opinion. Take yourself seriously as a researcher who draws conclusions based on the material and its evaluation. This is what distinguishes an academic perspective from a personal view. The results you are producing should be valid for everyone. The words "I" and "my" (as well as "we" and "our") should therefore be banned from a research paper.

### Error #6: Subscribing to Statements from Secondary Literature Without Reflection, Usage of Obsolete Sources

Do not be mistaken: secondary literature was quoted and paraphrased correctly. So everything is fine? Think again. Is writing epigrammes really the mark of a bad writer? Do all women novelists corrupt society? The source by C.S. Lewis is almost a century old, it is safe to say that Lewis' views are obsolete in literary criticism today. Some critical evaluation of the source would be indicated if one was inclined to use it at all. Describe Lewis' position and contrast it with your own criticism, but do not copy statements from an outdated source only because it was printed that way a long time ago. Academic writing is discussion and reflection. Think about what you read, dare to challenge the views of others.

A paper of twelve pages can never cover the whole history of research of a topic. What it should mirror is the current state of research. Your sources should not be older than ten to 15 years. Most libraries have separate shelves for their latest acquisitions. Better refrain from using books which were published when your grandmother was in primary school.

### Error #7: Colloquial Language

> Lizzy and Jane are hot chicks.
> At the end of the day, Satan's just fed up with God, the Son, the angels, etc.

Aim for a neutral, objective tone. Contractions such as "Satan's" instead of "Satan is", "can't" or "don't" instead of "cannot" or "do not" are uncommon in written English. Enumerations should not be cut off with "etc.". Start with "for example" instead and provide a few aspects.

## Error #8: Lack of Expert Definitions

A definition such as Samuel Johnson's may be used as a catch-phrase at the beginning of your introduction or your body of theory. It is, however, unsuitable as an academic definition of the term 'satire': firstly, it was taken from the *Encyclopaedia Britannica*, not a glossary of literary terms; secondly, it is an aphorism, not a formal description of criteria. Furthermore, the definition does not take into account that satire can be both a literary genre (formal verse satire) and a mode of writing (within another genre). Encyclopaedias and lexicon articles count among academic sources, providing a rough overview for a first impression of a term. This should only be the first step. If expert knowledge from a particular field is required, look up the term in glossaries and handbooks, explore the etymology of the word, look for studies concerning genre. The more precise your idea of the definition is, the easier it will be to apply in your written work. If you only have a vague conception of the central terms of your topic, your analysis will be superficial.

## Error #9: Missing Sources, Unintentional Plagiarism, Anachronism

> Mary Wollstonecraft faced a fundamental problem in writing her *Vindication of the Rights of Woman*: language. In the eighteenth century, there was **no genuine female language** to express women's concerns in their very own language, **linked to female sexuality**. Therefore, Wollstonecraft had to argue in terms of **male logic**, using **marginalizing, patriarchal language and vocabulary**.

The terms in bold face are neither explained nor defined. The author uses the arguments brought forward by poststructual feminists (Cixous, Irigaray, Kristeva) without indicating them as sources. Any evidence from secondary literature (publications on feminism and writing, if this is not the main topic of the paper, a handbook on literary theory may suffice[20]) is re-

---

[20]    You can find a list of suitable books in the appendix to this volume.

quired; suitable quotes by Cixous and some commentary should be added. Besides, the phrasing is problematic: "Mary Wollstonecraft faced a fundamental problem"; given that the argument of language is introduced by feminists 150 years after Wollstonecraft, it seems at the very least doubtful if Wollstonecraft ever perceived language as a problem. The poststructuralist feminists faced severe criticism as well, which is not even mentioned, but their line of argument is taken for granted by the author of the paper.

Separate your own ideas from those of others at all times. Clarify if you have only quoted one last sentence, or if you have paraphrased the whole train of thought.

### Error #10: Mindreading, Intentionalism

No matter if Mary Shelley was a passionate hiker, it cannot be read into her novel *Frankenstein*. It is pure speculation. Not only does the author ignore Burke's concept of the Sublime as a theoretical foundation of landscape description in many Gothic novels, but he also refers to *l'art pour l'art* (without providing so much as a footnote), the paradigm of aestheticism which did not rise to prominence until many years after Shelley's death in 1851. Furthermore, the author simply assumes that Shelley "intended" to embellish her novel without reflecting the problematic nature of intentionalist approaches to literature (*cf.* Wimsatt und Beardsley, *intentional fallacy*).

### Error #11: The J.K. Rowling Complex

> Mary Shelley's novel *Frankenstein* criticizes the dishonesty and the *hubris* of the scientist. **If Victor Frankenstein had immediately confessed** his creation to his friend Henry Clerval, they could have pursued the Creature together. **They might even have** prevented the Creature's revenge and integrated it into society, **which would have added a completely new twist to the plot.**

Basically, academia thrives on creative and original ideas – you are welcome to think outside the box. This does not mean, however, that you should write a new version of the primary text. In the highly unlikely event that you are the next J.K. Rowling, your academic paper is simply the wrong place to demonstrate it. Focus on analyzing what is at hand.

### Error #12: Anachronisms

"The Shadow in the Rose Garden" by D.H. Lawrence was published in November 1914, shortly after the outbreak of World War I (Britain declared war on Germany in August). The war the soldier is returning from is the Boer War, fought between the British Empire and the two Boer states in Africa.

As a lot of modernist literature attempts to deal with the trauma of World War I, we automatically relate any texts from that period to these events. It is generally a good idea to look up historical contexts before drawing such conclusions. It happens to the best of us: In Shakespeare's *Julius Caesar*, set in 44 BC, Cassius says that "The clock hath stricken three" (2.1.192).[21] The earliest record of a weight-driven mechanical clock dates back to 1283 AD.[22]

### Exercises

### Exercise 7.1: Titles in Bibliographies

Imagine you want to use the following titles in your bibliography. Which words would you need to capitalize?

a) the war of the worlds
b) the old man and the sea
c) the house on mango street

---

[21]   William Shakespeare, *Julius Caesar*. Ed. David Daniell. The Arden Shakespeare, Third Series (London: A&C Black, 1998).

[22]   William J.H. Andrewes, "A Chronicle of Timekeeping". *Scientific American*, 1 Feb 2006. Web. 29 Sept 2019. <https://www.scientificamerican.com/article/a-chronicle-of-timekeeping-2006-02/>.

d) staying on
e) men without women
f) nineteen eighty-four

## Exercise 7.2: Now You Be the Lecturer!

Read the following examples regarding structure of argument, good academic practice, style, and language. You do not need to be familiar with the primary texts to be able to judge the quality of these paragraphs. Are they convincing? Do you feel you know more about the topic after reading the paragraph? Why (not)? What would you change?

a) **From the Introduction: John Fowles, *The French Lieutenant's Woman***

In his novel *The French Lieutenant's Woman*, John Fowles shows how the liberated woman Sarah is outlawed by the Victorians due to their strict moral standards. In late Victorianism, society was very religious, and any form of sexuality was frowned upon. Sarah seems more like a modern woman: she wants to pursue a career of her own and is not fixated on marriage and having children. She is like the women in contemporary society, who are no longer disadvantaged.

b) **From the Analytical Part: The Function of Intertextuality in John Fowles, *The Collector***

Frederick Clegg seems to be an isolated, psychologically disturbed person. He has not received much affection from his family, which may have been detrimental to his process of development and maturity. It remains in the dark whether there is a real chance for Miranda, whom he has kidnapped, to fall in love with him, or whether Frederick will succumb to his distorted perception and self-deceptive tendencies.

c) **From the Conclusion: The Function of Intertextuality in John Fowles, *The Collector***

All in all, it can be concluded that with *The Collector*, John Fowles has created an original novel which is capable of surprise. This impression is confirmed by the intertextual references to Shakespeare's *The Tempest*. What is most terrifying about the novel is its ending, in which readers are left alone to wonder who is going to be the protagonist's next victim and if he will eventually be arrested.

d) **From the Conclusion: Concepts of Masculinity in *Othello***

Obviously, there are several aspects of research which could not be fully acknowledged in this research paper. There are more male characters in Shakespeare's drama which could have been considered, such as Brabantio, Roderigo, and Cassio. The goal of this paper, discussing concepts of masculinity in Othello, was achieved by analyzing Iago and Othello, however, this analysis might be continued in exploring more characters in depth.

# Chapter 8: Single White Quotation Seeks Same

It is an essential characteristic of an academic text that you give evidence for every argument, a process in which one's own considerations must be clearly separated from those of others. For this purpose, scholars distinguish between two basic options of integrating ideas into one's own work: paraphrase and quotation.

## 8.1 Formally Correct Citation

In a paraphrase, you reproduce the content of someone else's text in your own words. Although you do not cite the source literally, the paraphrase contains the original work of another scholar. Therefore, the source must be documented.

### Example: Primary Source

What matters therefore in the historical novel is not the re-telling of great historical events, but the poetic awakening of the people who figured in those events. What matters is that we should re-experience the social and human motives which led men to think, feel and act just as they did in historical reality.[1]

**WRONG (Plagiarism):** Integrating the text without providing any sources:

> In contrast to historiography as a science, which is based on rational facts, the historical novel focusses on psychological conditions and individual experience of history. Therefore, what matters in the historical novel is not the re-telling of great historical events, but the poetic

---

[1] Georg Lukács, *The Historical Novel*. Trans. Hannah and Stanley Mitchell (Boston: Beacon, 1963), 42.

awakening of the people who figured in those events. What matters is that we should re-experience the social and human motives which led men to think, feel and act just as they did in historical reality. This idea is often expressed in the analysis of Sir Walter Scott's novels.

The author of this paper has mixed up his or her own ideas with those expressed by Lukács. Using quotations and paraphrases without proper documentation is **plagiarism** and will lead to your paper being rejected.

### CORRECT: Paraphrase with documented source:

In contrast to historiography as a science, which is based on rational facts, the historical novel focuses on psychological conditions and individual experience of history. According to Georg Lukács, the historical novel should not simply be an account of important historical contexts (51). Its purpose is to help people in the present understand why the protagonists of past events acted the way they did (*ibid*.). Lukács uses this definition to analyse the novels of Sir Walter Scott.

### CORRECT: Quotation with documented source:

In contrast to historiography as a science, which is based on rational facts, the historical novel focusses on psychological conditions and individual experience of history:

> What matters therefore in the historical novel is not the re-telling of great historical events, but the poetic awakening of the people who figured in those events. What matters is that we should re-experience the social and human motives which led men to think, feel and act just as they did in historical reality (Lukács 51).

Lukács uses this definition to analyse the novels of Sir Walter Scott.

**Quotations** shorter than a) MLA7: three lines or b) MLA8: three lines of verse or four lines of prose are integrated into the text in double quotation marks (full stops, commas and semicolons should be after the author-page indication of the source in brackets). Longer quotations should be indented by

0.5 inch (1 cm) from the left margin without quotation marks (this is called a block quote).

To clarify where your own ideas start, you have to **document your sources for every single idea you take from other people's works** – everything else is plagiarism, even if you add the source somewhere at the bottom of the page or three pages later.

In academia, several Latin abbreviations are widely used for ideas taken from the same source. These are:

- *ibid*.: Latin *ibidem*, "in the same place", meaning on the same page as your last quote
- *op. cit*. (followed by page number): Latin *opere citato*, "in the work just cited", meaning in the same work as your last quote, but on a different page. Some scholars also use *ibid*., followed by a page number instead of *op. cit*.
- *passim*: Latin "here and there", preceded by page number; this means the same idea is expressed in many different places of a work, so you only document the first occurrence.

The use of these Latin abbreviations, however, is controversial in academia today.[2] If you use *ibid*. or *op. cit*. and you insert a new quotation in between the entry it refers to later, your *ibid*. is no longer correct, so double-check your paper for such errors.

Latin abbreviations which are perfectly acceptable (and often expected) in scholarly writing in English are *e.g.* (*exempli gratia*, for example), *i.e.* (*id est*, that is, for providing a definition or stating an equivalence), *cf.* (*confer*, compare,

---

[2]    Burkhard Moennighoff and Eckhardt Meyer-Krentler regard these abbreviations as "embarrassing" and have called their use "a superfluous scholarly kind of display behaviour". *Cf. Arbeitstechniken Literaturwissenschaft* (München: Fink/UTB, 2013), 56.

which points the reader to a source giving a different view from the one just expressed).[3]

Citations have to be copied without changing neologisms, typos, orthographic errors, or uncommon varieties of spelling. By placing [*sic!*] behind your quote, you demonstrate that you are aware that this is not how you would commonly spell the word without changing your source. Omitting parts of a quote is permitted as long as you provide three dots or three dots in brackets (for whole lines omitted in poetry, provide a whole line of dots). Example:

> Do vampyres [*sic!*] play chess? Were there vampyre dorks? How about Barbie-like vampyre cheerleaders? Did any vampyres play in the band? […] Or were they all those freaky Goth kids who didn't like to bathe much? Was I going to turn into a Goth kid? I didn't particularly like wearing black, at least not exclusively.[4]

In the novel quoted above, the word 'vampyre' is consistently written with a 'y', an alternative spelling that occurred at the same time as 'vampire', but is no longer common today. P.C. and Kristin Cast use this spelling as a stylistic device. Since this can seem like a typo to someone who is not familiar with the novels, a [*sic!*] is useful to avoid misunderstandings. It is not reasonable, however, to mark every archaic word with a [*sic!*] when working with a Shakespeare play. An imaginary peer-group must be at least familiar enough with Elizabethan English to know that it differs significantly from modern English in many ways. The text may not be altered unless it is absolutely necessary, and these changes must be marked. Such changes may include: supplementary explanations necessary to understanding, adaptation of upper and lower case

---

[3]    Some styles (not including MLA style) mark all paraphrases consequently using *cf.*, as to distinguish them from direct citations. For more examples, see "Latin Terms and Abbreviations". *Writing Center University of North Carolina at Chapel Hill*. Web. 19 August 2019. <https://writingcenter.unc.edu/tips-and-tools/latin-terms-and-abbreviations>.

[4]    P.C. and Kristin Cast, *Marked* (New York: St Martin's Press, 2007), 5.

to the context (the changed letter is placed in square brackets), emphasis on accentuation.[5] Have a look at the following passage from Henry Fielding's *Joseph Andrews* (1742), in which a maid at an inn ensures that Joseph receives medical attention after he has been attacked by robbers:

> The wench soon got Joseph to bed, and promised to use her interest to borrow him a shirt; but imagining, as she afterwards said, by his being so bloody, that he must be a dead man, she ran with all speed to hasten the surgeon, who was more than half drest, apprehending that the coach had been overturned, and some gentleman or lady hurt. As soon as the wench had informed him at his window that it was a poor foot-passenger who had been stripped of all he had, and almost murdered, he chid her for disturbing him so early, slipped off his clothes again, and very quietly returned to bed and to sleep.[6]

If you quote only the second part of the passage, you need to ensure your readers understand who is reacting so dismissively, for example with a statement in parentheses:

> As soon as the wench had informed him [the surgeon] at his window that it was a poor foot-passenger who had been stripped of all he had, and almost murdered, he chid her for disturbing him so early (Fielding 44).

When the quote starts in mid-sentence, alter the first letter:

> [S]he ran with all speed to hasten the surgeon, who was more than half drest, apprehending that the coach had been overturned, and some gentleman or lady hurt (Fielding 44).

If you want to emphasize something, such as "a poor foot-passenger", italicize it:

> As soon as the wench had informed him at his window that it was *a poor foot-passenger* who had been stripped of all he had, and almost murdered, he chid her for disturbing him so early, slipped off his clothes again, and very quietly returned to bed and to sleep (Fielding 44, emphasis added).

---

[5]    Occasionally, for reasons of legibility, publishers waive such markers.

[6]    Henry Fielding, *Joseph Andrews. With* Shamela *and Related Writings*. A Norton Critical Edition. Ed. Homer Goldberg (New York and London: Norton, 1987), 44.

## 8.2 Documenting Sources in Literary and Cultural Studies

The form of documentation differs depending on which style (*e.g.* MLA style, Chicago style) is preferred at your department. When in doubt, ask your lecturers about the preferred citation method. Apply the method you have chosen consistently. The Modern Language Association recommends the following form of documentation:

> The difficulty in the study of the Robin Hood tradition lies in the "interaction between fictive text and social context" (Singman 4), a line that appears to be rather difficult to draw.

It is the shortest way of documenting a source, indicating the surname of the author followed by the page number.[7]

This method, however, often renders it difficult to read a paragraph if it contains several references, since the flow of your reading is constantly interrupted. Therefore, it is a sensible, permissible alternative in the humanities to place the bibliographic record within a footnote:

> The difficulty in the study of the Robin Hood tradition lies in the "interaction between fictive text and social context",[1] a line that appears to be rather difficult to draw.

---

[1]  Jeffrey L. Singman, *Robin Hood: The Shaping of A Legend* (Westport: Greenwood, 1998), 4.

Please note how the format of the footnote differs from that of your bibliography at the end of your paper:

**Bibliography:** Singman, Jeffrey L. *Robin Hood: The Shaping of a Legend*. Westport: Greenwood, 1998.

**Footnote:** Jeffrey L. Singman, *Robin Hood: The Shaping of a Legend* (Westport: Greenwood, 1998), 4.

**Unlike your bibliography**, the footnote will **first** mention the author's **first name** ('Jeffrey L. Singman', not 'Singman,

---

[7]  Some style sheets require author and page to be separated by a comma.

Jeffrey L.'). The place of publication, publisher and year of publication are provided in brackets.

Such a detailed specification, however, is only required when a work is first mentioned. For all following citations, the so-called short title procedure is used:

---

[2]  Singman, *Robin Hood*, 4.

If you quote lots of secondary sources, as is the case in lengthy bodies of theory in literary and cultural studies, use phrases containing the author's name very sparingly, such as "In this context, Singman points out that…", for example if you compare two opposing positions of two authors with each other. Too many (sometimes quite complex) names interfere with the reading. A good alternative is to use neutral phrases: "In this context, it has to be considered that.." and to save the name of the author for documentation. Of course, you will still pay attention to the clear separation of your own thoughts and other people's ideas. "Famous" names which your readers will be familiar with (such as Freud and Shakespeare) can be mentioned in the text. The first time you mention them, use the full name ("William Shakespeare"). Academic degrees or other titles are completely omitted; write "Samuel Johnson" instead of "Dr Johnson".

**Second-hand quotes** (you quote Jones, who in turn quotes from a book by Smith) are only permissible if the original source is not available (for example, if Smith's book is out of print and cannot be obtained at all or on time via interlibrary loan). You must at least provide credible evidence of this in a footnote. Otherwise, indirect quotations are not regarded as good academic practice. You are obliged to research the original source if it is possible.

**Documenting Primary Literature:** If you have just one primary text, it is sufficient to place the page number in brackets after the quotation:

> Jane Austen's novel *Pride and Prejudice* starts with the following words: "It is a truth universally acknowledged that a single man in possession of a good fortune must be in want of a wife" (1).

If you have several primary texts to compare, for each text you enter a so-called **scribal abbreviation** for the full title, followed by the page number. If your primary text is not part of the larger work, scribal abbreviations must be in italics as well:

> The importance of financial independence in Austen's novels becomes evident in the phrasing of their first sentences: "a single man in possession of a good fortune must be in want of a wife" (*PP* 1), Sir Thomas Betram of Mansfield Park has a "handsome house and large income" (*MP* 1).

## 8.3 Documenting Sources in Linguistics

In linguistics, bibliographic records are not normally provided in footnotes. The author's name, the year of publication and the page number are mandatory. The latter two can be placed directly behind the author's name:

Option 1:

> Baron-Cohen (1995, 3) therefore claims that all human beings permanently try to explain the thought processes of other cognitive agents, *i.e.* that every human being is basically constantly imvolved in a process of *mindreading* without being aware of it.

Option 2:

> "We mindread all the time, effortlessly, automatically, and mostly unconsciously. That is, we are often not even aware we are doing it" (Baron-Cohen 1995, 3).

To be able to file the references from the text as quickly as possible under the corresponding bibliographic entries in your bibliography, the bibliography of a paper in linguistics also has to be structured in a different way. Entries begin with the name of the author, followed directly by the year of publication.

> Baron-Cohen, Simon (1997). *Mindblindness*. Cambridge, MA: MIT Press.

Article in an anthology:

> Wilson, Margo & Martin Daly (1992). "The Man Who Mistook his Wife for a Chattel". In Jerome Barkow, Leda Cosmides, John Tooby (ed.), *The Adapted Mind.* Oxford: OUP, 289-322.

The commercial "&" (and) as well as the addition "In:" for anthologies are more common to linguistics than literary and cultural studies.

## 8.4 Using Quotations Efficiently

A pointed quote from secondary literature can be an efficient way to support your own argument. It may have the opposite effect, however, if the quotation is left to speak for itself without any explanatory remarks; in the worst case, an entire short chapter may consist only of the quotation.[8]

### WRONG: Quote replaces own statements, stands isolated

#### 1.1 Science in H.G. Wells, *The Island of Doctor Moreau*

> And yet this extraordinary branch of knowledge has never been sought as an end, and systematically, by modern investigators, until I took it up! Some at least of the inquisitors must have had a touch of scien-

---

[8]    The following examples were adapted from Simone Broders, "'A Serpent to Sting You' – The Medical Practitioner Caught Between Curiosity and Monstrosity. Frankenstein, Jekyll, Moreau", *The Writing Cure. Literature and Medicine in Context*, ed. Alexandra Lembert-Heidenreich, Jarmila Mildorf (Münster: LIT, 2013), 55-76.

tific curiosity… […] And here I have wasted a day saving your life, and now I am wasting an hour explaining myself (*IDM*, 72-3).

**1.2 Science in R.L. Stevenson, *Strange Case of Doctor Jekyll and Mr Hyde***

## RIGHT: Quotation supplements and supports own statements

Moreau is so immersed in his own curiosity that it is a mystery to him how other scientists may be reluctant to cross that line:

And yet this extraordinary branch of knowledge has never been sought as an end, and systematically, by modern investigators, until I took it up! Some at least of the inquisitors must have had a touch of scientific curiosity… […] And here I have wasted a day saving your life, and now I am wasting an hour explaining myself (*IDM*, 72-3).

The quotation demonstrates how Moreau becomes detached from his own humanity through his scientific pursuit. Moreau sees himself in the role of the creator, whose "ways are unfathomable" and who has no need to justify himself. He draws parallels between his creation and the creation of Christianity, as John Bachelor points out …

Quotations can never speak for themselves, you must provide contexts, present opposing views, and critically judge whether the person quoted is right at all. It is extremely problematic to adopt positions without criticism, especially if they are outdated or extremely controversial. Show that you have understood what you have read and that you are able to balance the pros and cons of the respective position in order to arrive at a well-founded academic opinion.

### Example:
The following argument examines the role of curiosity in the literary character of the medical scientist from different angles.

### Step 1: Presenting the first theoretical position

Bacon is convinced that man has to learn about both the spiritual and the material world to be ultimately saved. His *Advancement of Learn-*

*ing* thus promotes a utilitarian view of science; everything that is subject to research must serve to improve man's standard of living and quality of life. Barbara Benedict observes that Bacon is also the first one to categorize the weaknesses of the scientist – among others envy, greed, vanity, obsession (Bacon, 147-8) –, yet he argues that those are either misconceptions of the profession, or weaknesses of individual scientists (Benedict 67). The true scientist, according to Bacon, is humble, virtuous, and concerned about other people's well-being. The English word 'curiosity' is thus closely related to *cura*, 'care', as well as to 'cure', 'remedy'.

Bacon's argumentation is presented and supported by secondary literature, an essay by Barbara Benedict. If the paragraph ends at this point, the statement is: "The scientist wants to be useful, scientific curiosity is therefore something good." That, however, is only Bacon's position. Therefore, another paragraph has to follow to represent the opposite view:

### Step 2: Representing the opposite position

Curiosity, however, is not always evaluated in a positive way even as medicine emerges as a science – as Hermann J. Real observes, stories of curious people falling victim to the sin of *hubris* are often those of scientists, and all too often, utilitarian justifications of curiosity "veil the personal will to knowledge with the ulterior motive of social service" (31).

In the end, critically compare the positions to come to some kind of conclusion. You do not have to take a side eventually, but your reasoning should serve to raise readers' awareness of the strengths and weaknesses of the respective position and formulate the conclusions from both points of view as clearly and as objectively as possible.

### Step 3: Critical consideration in the light of one's own topic :

Both of these aspects of curiosity, the philanthropic care for others and the insatiable desire to know, are inherent in the literary character of the physician – the respectable medical practitioner vying for dominance with the ambitious researcher; the desire to relieve pain and suffering opposes the secret longing for the fame that goes with an epoch-making discovery.

The purpose of quotations is to help you prove your own theories and reasoning. Under no circumstance, however, can they replace your own work. If you submit a pastiche of quotations from secondary literature with no added value to your paper, you will not pass the course. In your academic writing, you should demonstrate your understanding of the principles of scholarly research, as the metaphor of the giants and dwarfs illustrates: the dwarfs (moderns) are standing on the shoulders of the giants (ancients).[9] In the same way, young scholars base their own research on the accomplishments of academics in the past.

## Exercises

### Exercise 8.1: Quotations. True or false?

a) Quotations of three lines of prose are embedded into the text with quotation marks.
b) Quotations of more than three lines of verse are separated from the text in a block quotation, using quotation marks.
c) All quotations must be italicized.
d) Typos or spelling mistakes in quotations may be corrected.
e) You should end a chapter with a concise quote from secondary literature.

---

[9]    The allegory of dwarfs and giants to describe the relationship between moderns and ancients has been attributed to Bernard of Chartres by John Salisbury:"He [Chartres] pointed out that we see more and farther than our predecessors, not because we have keener vision or greater height, but because we are lifted up and borne aloft on their gigantic stature". Daniel Doyle MacGarry, *The Metalogicon of John Salisbury: A Twelfth-Century Defense of the Verbal and Logical Arts of the Trivium* (Berkeley, CA: University of California Press, 1955), 167.

f) Second-hand quotations (Stoker in Auerbach 44) are always permitted.
g) Words in quotations may be omitted, but have to be marked as such.
h) If you start a quotation in the middle of a sentence, you may change the upper-case letter to an lower-case letter without marking it.

### Exercise 8.2: Latin, Anyone?

Complete the following text by adding a suitable Latin abbreviation: *cf., e.g., ibid., i.e., [sic!]*

Thomas Spence, born in Newcastle upon Tyne in 1750, was the son of Scottish parents and one of nineteen children (Mackenzie 399-400). His father, a netmaker, being a deeply religious man, insisted on his sons learning to read from the Bible (???). Spence's convictions were influenced by the Glassite sect, ??? a Protestant group known for its advocacy of communal ownership of property.

Unlike other eighteenth-century philosophers with an upper-class upbringing, ??? William Godwin, Spence addressed his texts to an audience comprised of peasants and craftsmen.

Human rights are established in Spence's 1803 *Constitution of Spensonia*: "Government is instituted to secure to man the enjoyment of his natural and impresceptable ??? rights" (166).

The economic independence of women from their husbands and fathers is one of the greatest advancements of Spence's political utopias. Some authors, however, argue that they still reflect the type of conservative, passive female behaviour characteristic of eighteenth-century English society (??? Duthille 21).

# Chapter 9: Preparing the Manuscript

Once you have successfully finished writing your paper, you are not done yet – you face a task that is often underestimated, but can be quite daunting: the transformation of a body of text into a neatly structured manuscript which adheres to precise stylistic guidelines, does not contain any typos nor coffee stains, and presents the results of your research in an appealing form. Reserve enough time for completing the manuscript – at least a week for a seminar paper, at least two weeks for a dissertation. As a rule, your university will require you to submit a physical manuscript with a signed affidavit, either as a bound copy or in a clip folder. They may also ask you to provide an additional electronic version as a PDF file on a CD, DVD or USB stick.

Remember Murphy's Law: if anything can possibly go wrong, it will. This is also true for your hardware, so do not start printing your manuscript half an hour before submission.

## 9.1 Why Bother with Style Sheets?

Adhering to strict stylistic guidelines when formatting your paper may seem pedantic. Granted: it takes some time and practice to get used to citations, footnotes, and bibliographic records, and at first glance, it may not matter much whether titles are underlined or formatted in italics. To most beginning students, formatting a paper according to a style sheet is a tedious, time-consuming task with no immediate use. Styles vary not only between the humanities and the sciences, but occasionally also within the same discipline, for example between English linguistics and literary studies. Standards are nonetheless useful tools, facilitating orientation and comprehension for your readers.

Using MLA Style properly makes it easier for readers to navigate and comprehend a text by providing familiar cues when referring to sources and borrowed information. Abiding by MLA standards as a writer will allow you to:

- Provide your readers with cues they can use to follow your ideas more efficiently and to locate information of interest to them.
- Allow readers to focus more on your ideas by not distracting them with unfamiliar or complicated formatting.
- Establish your credibility or ethos in the field by demonstrating an awareness of your audience and their needs as fellow researchers (particularly concerning the citing of references).[1]

With a consistent style your readers are familiar with, it is evident where you have developed your own line of argument and which parts have been quoted from other authors. Both your readers and yourself can easily relocate a specific passage in the text. Adhering to a style sheet, you show respect for other people's achievements and consideration of your addressees.

"But I'm just a student! Probably no other scholar is ever going to read my paper!"

First of all, you have no way of knowing what you might or might not publish later in life. Publishers have style sheets as well, and manuscripts failing to adhere to them will be returned without further ado. If you become a teacher, someone may ask you to contribute to a textbook. If you compile worksheets and other materials for your pupils, you have to make sure they are well-structured and consistent. Inconsistent materials will confuse learners and will distract them from the content they are supposed to study.

Secondly, points will be taken off for formatting errors for a good reason: the longer you are working on your paper, the more important the presentation of your manuscript be-

---

[1]    "MLA Overview and Workshop". *OWL Purdue University Writing Lab.* Web. 14 August 2019. <https://owl.purdue.edu/owl/research_and_citation/mla_style/mla_overview_and_workshop.html>.

comes. Otherwise, you may lose track of your own golden thread. Furthermore, a speedy correction of papers is in your best interest, as you may need the results as a prerequisite for an advanced seminar, to apply for a grant, or register for exams. Formal deviations render it more difficult to compare seminar papers within the same class – you may not be able to tell immediately if someone has exceeded the page limit if they format their paper in the wrong font and size. Suggestions and corrections are difficult to add when the author of the paper has not left any margins. As a result, corrections will take up more time – time that would be better spent on feedback on your line of argument.

Look up guidelines and cases not covered in this book. Prepare your manuscript with care and accuracy. Next to content and evaluation of sources, form is one of the central criteria for assessment. If one of the three areas is marked with a 'fail', the whole paper may not be above a mere 'pass' grade, or, depending on your university's exam regulations, your work may be turned down for formal reasons.

You are not sure how to set the margins of a document or move a tab stop? You have never inserted an image into a text and think a thesaurus is related to a Tyrannosaurus Rex? If so, familiarize yourself with a word processing programme. Workshops especially for students are offered regularly at most universities.

Most word processing programmes are based on the principle of WYSIWYG, short for "What you see is what you get" – what is displayed on your screen corresponds to the printed page. You can click on an element on your screen and directly change its appearance. An alternative to WYSIWYG the document preparation system LaTeX (pronounced (/ˈlɑːtɛx/, /x/ as in 'Lo**ch** Ness'), which runs on top of the typesetting system TeX. Formatting in LaTeX is not done by clicking a symbol on a ribbon or toolbar, but by editing code. You cannot see the changes to your document directly, but you can display a preview. A LaTeX document might look like this:

```
\documentclass{book}
\title{Academic Skills}
\subtitle{An Introduction for English and American Studies}
\author{Simone Broders}
\date{October 2019}
\begin{document}
  \maketitle
  How to be curious – this is where your text begins
\end{document}
```

LaTex is very popular in science and technology because the typesetting of complex mathematical formulas is much easier than in a WYSIWYG system. In addition to that, LaTex tends to be more stable than most WYSIWYG programmes with large documents, say, a PhD thesis. More advantages of LaTex are the automatic creation of bibliographies and indexes, and the typesetting for ancient philologies, with additional packages available.[2] Do not hesitate to try something new, even though LaTex is not as widely used in the humanities; however, do not let your friend who is studying computer science persuade you that it is impossible to create a good manuscript in WYSIWYG software. You should be familiar with one way of preparing documents, but which one you choose is entirely up to you.

Next to word processing software, many scholars work with programmes for reference management and knowledge organization such as *Citavi*, *Docear*, *Zotero*, *RefWorks*, and *EndNote*. Think of a reference management system as a digital card box, as were used in libraries before digital catalogues became available.[3]

---

[2]    For more information, *cf*. "An Introduction to LaTex". *LaTex – A Document Preparation System*. Web. 15 Aug 2019. <https://www.latex-project.org/>.

[3]    Isabella Ettner, Konstanze Söllner, "Nie wieder abtippen! Der richtige Umgang mit Literaturverwaltungsprogrammen". *Universitätsbibliothek Ludwig-*

These programmes automatically recognize the ISBN number of a publication, so you will not have to enter bibliographic information manually, such as title, author, publisher. The list of works cited is then generated automatically according to the chosen style of citation, *e.g.* MLA, APA, or Chicago.[4] Typos and errors caused by copying, such as the easy mistake of transforming the "Johns Hopkins University" into "John Hopkins University", can easily be avoided. You should, however, be able to create a list of works cited manually for several reasons. Your department may still be using an older version of the chosen style, or have its own style sheet with modifications to the official style. Furthermore, the conventions of a particular style also apply to the text of your paper, and there is no programme available as of date that will format a whole paper for you. More importantly still, you should be familiar with the stylistic conventions of the subject you study. Think of it as a useful exercise. Would you have learnt your tables if your primary school teacher had allowed you to use a pocket calculator in grade 1?

## 9.2 MLA Style

As the style guidelines of the *MLA* have become standard procedure for the submission of research papers in modern languages, the most important characteristics of MLA style will be summarized briefly. As there is a guideline for every formatting problem, this overview will not save you the trouble of consulting the official *MLA Handbook* by Joseph Gibaldi to look up the particulars.

---

*Maximilians-Universität München*. Web. 14 April 2013.
<http://www.ub.uni-muenchen.de/fileadmin/dokumente/pdf/Skript_Citavi_EndNote.pdf>.
[4]    *Ibid*.

In the 8th edition, however, there have been substantial changes to MLA style, some of which (such as dropping the place of publication from the bibliographical record, or no longer requiring students to give the complete URL of an internet source) have been controversially discussed or even downright rejected by some departments. Please make sure whether your department requires you to use

Joseph Gibaldi, *MLA Handbook for Writers of Research Papers*, 7th edition (New York: MLA, 2009), henceforth referred to as **"MLA7", *OR***

Joseph Gibaldi, *MLA Handbook*, 8th edition (New York: MLA, 2016), henceforth referred to as **"MLA8".** You will find an overview of the most important changes in the respective parts of this chapter.

You can download a sample paper formatted completely in MLA8 at the *OWL Purdue University Writing Lab*.[5] **Please note that your department may have adapted some aspects of MLA style for practical reasons,** such as requiring you to add a title page containing additional information, such as your contact data, field and year of study, and date of submission. It is a wide-spread convention to represent block quotes single-spaced and in a font size 1–2 point smaller than the text of your paper, whereas the MLA suggests double-spaced block quotes the same size as your text. Check your departmental home page for information and individual style sheets. A core element of MLA style is the distinction between larger and shorter works.

'**Larger Works'.** Works are considered 'larger' if they do not appear inside another work, but are published separately, standing by themselves, such as novels, dramas, anthologies, journals, or collections of essays. Titles of 'larger works' are

---

[5]   Elizabeth L. Angeli, "Toward a Recovery of Nineteenth-Century Farming Handbooks". *Purdue University*. 12 August 2019. <https://owl.purdue.edu/owl/research_and_citation/mla_style/mla_formatting_and_style_guide/documents/20180702110400_747-2.pdf>.

formatted in *italics* (back in the age of typewriters, they used to be underlined. Note that underlining is no longer acceptable in MLA style). Give the last and first name of the author, the title of the work, along with publisher and year of publication. MLA7 also requires the place of publication and the medium (the most common types being print, web, TV, DVD). When indicating the publisher, leave out any additions such as "Publishing" or "Limited". [6]

> MLA7: Eco, Umberto. *The Name of the Rose.* London: Vintage, 2004. Print.
> MLA 8: Eco, Umberto. *The Name of the Rose*. Vintage, 2004.

If your source is not a first edition, add the number of the edition after the title ("3rd ed.") in MLA8. In MLA7, the edition is displayed superscript with smaller digits ($^3$2004).

**'Smaller Works'.** Works are considered 'smaller' if they are published within a larger work, such as a poem or short story in an anthology, an article in a book, journal or on a website. Titles of 'smaller' works are placed in double quotation marks. The title of the larger work is formatted in italics. For the smaller work, the exact page numbers are given.

> MLA7: Benedict, Barbara. "The Mad Scientist: The Creation of a Literary Stereotype". *Imagining the Sciences: Expressions of New Knowledge in the 'Long' Eighteenth Century*. Ed. Robert C. Leitz III, and Kevin L. Cope. New York: AMS, 2004. 59-107. Print.
> MLA8: Benedict, Barbara. "The Mad Scientist: The Creation of a Literary Stereotype". *Imagining the Sciences:Expressions of New Knowledge in the 'Long' Eighteenth Century*, edited by Robert C. Leitz III and Kevin L. Cope, AMS, 2004, pp. 59-107.

Note that in MLA8, the abbreviation "ed." has been replaced by "edited by", and page numbers are preceded by "p." (one page) or "pp." (more than one page).

---

[6]   Abbreviate "University Press" as"UP" only if there is no additional word in between, *i.e.* "Oxford UP","Cambridge UP (or, in these cases, even OUP, CUP)", but "University of Chicago Press" (not "U of Chicago P").

If a book or article was written or edited by more than one individual, it is listed under the last name of the first author or editor. For each additional author or publisher, list the first name first – not: "Cottegnies, Line, Parageau, Sandrine, and Thompson, John J.", but "Cottegnies, Line, Sandrine Parageau, and John J. Thompson".

> MLA 7: Cottegnies, Line, Sandrine Parageau, and John J. Thompson, eds. *Women and Curiosity in Early Modern England and France*. Leiden: Brill, 2016. Print.
> MLA 8: Cottegnies, Line, *e.a., editors. Women and Curiosity in Early Modern England and France*. Brill, 2016.

In MLA8, only the first author or editor is listed. If there are two or more authors, all subsequent authors are subsumed under *e.a.* (*et alii*, and others).

**Articles in scholarly journals:**
Bibliographic entries for articles in scholarly journals contain the number, the volume (if there are several volumes), the year of publication, and the page numbers.

> MLA7: Gunby, Ingrid. "History in Rags: Adam Thorpe's Reworking of England's National Past". *Contemporary Literature* 44/1 (Spring, 2003): 47-72. Print.
> MLA8: Gunby, Ingrid. "History in Rags: Adam Thorpe's Reworking of England's National Past". *Contemporary Literature,* vol. 44, no. 1, 2003, pp. 47-72.

**Articles from the Internet:**

> MLA7: "History". *The Royal Society*. Web. 27 February 2016. <https://royalsociety.org/about-us/history>.
> MLA8: "History". *The Royal Society,* 27 Feb 2016, https://royalsociety.org/about-us/history.

Articles are considered as part of a larger work, *i.e.* a website, an online journal, or an organization. The date when you accessed the source is an optional element according to MLA8 (as is the date of original publication), however, it may help your readers determine which version you consulted.

### Films and TV Series:

Films which have not been released on DVD or BlueRay yet:

> MLA7: *Call of the Wild*. Dir. Chris Sanders. Perf. Karen Gillan, Bradley Whitford, Harrison Ford. 3 Arts Entertainment, Twentieth-Century Fox, 2020. Film.
> MLA8: *Call of the Wild*. Directed by Chris Sanders, performances by Karen Gillan, Bradley Whitford, and Harrison Ford, 3 Arts Entertainment, Twentieth-Century Fox, 2020.

Contributors such as creators, writers, and performers are optional elements, however, they may help your reader distinguish different versions of frequently adapted materials such as Jack London's *Call of the Wild*.

For films which have been released on DVD or BlueRay, the exact release information is required:

> MLA 7: *Titanic. Standard Edition, 2 Discs.* Dir. James Cameron. Perf. Leonardo DiCaprio, Billy Zane, Kate Winslet. Twentieth-Century Fox Home Entertainment, 2012. DVD.
> MI A8: *Titanic. Standard Edition, 2 Discs.* Directed by James Cameron, performances by Leonardo DiCaprio, Billy Zane, Kate Winslet, Twentieth-Century Fox Home Entertainment, 2012.

Episodes of a TV series which have been aired on television, but not released have to contain the title of the episode, the title of the series, as well as the production company, the station and air date.

> MLA7: "1995". *The Loudest Voice*. Blumhouse Television. Showtime, 30 June 2019. TV.
> MLA8: "1995". *The Loudest Voice*. Blumhouse Television. Showtime, 30 June 2019.

If a TV series has been released, document the version you have watched in your list of works cited for MLA7, but not for MLA8:

MLA7: "Conversations with Dead People". *Buffy the Vampire Slayer Season 7 (New Packaging).* Writ. Jane Espenson and Drew Goddard. Dir. Nick Marck. Twentieth-Century Fox, 2011. DVD.

MLA8: "Conversations with Dead People". *Buffy the Vampire Slayer,* created by Joss Whedon, preformance by Sarah Michelle Gellar, season 7, episode 7, Mutant Enemy, 2011.

To find out who the writers and directors of individual episodes were, you can check out the credits of the episode or the *Internet Movie Database.* In times of streaming and online content, a source may belong to more than one container (for example, a TV series may be released at a streaming service as well as being released on DVD). Please check the style sheet of your department or the official *MLA Handbook* for further details and cases not covered here.

## 9.3 Checklist: Formatting Guidelines at a Glance

- **Margins.** In every style sheet, there are fixed guidelines for margins (look at the style sheet available from your department, or consult the official handbooks) which you should set in your word processing programme. In official MLA style, margins should be set to 1 inch (2.54 cm) on all sides. For student papers, the department may require wider margins to allow enough space for corrections, such as top and bottom: 0.78 inch (2 cm), left: 0.98 inch (2.5 cm), right: 1.38 inch (3.5 cm).
- **Font.** Font type and size are often compulsory. Elegant handwriting or original comic fonts are all very well for a birthday card, but inappropriate for academic papers. Popular fonts in research papers are Times New Roman 12 pt and Arial 11 pt (depending on the style used, block quotes may be smaller than the rest of the text). For lengthy passages of text in print, serif fonts such as Times New Roman have traditionally been credited with increased

readability.[7] Do not mix serif fonts with sans-serif fonts within the same document.

- **Use justification.**[8] Your word processing software will have a button to automatically apply justification to all pages of your paper. Example (see p. 9, note 1):
Justified margin (left) vs. ragged margin (right):

| | |
|---|---|
| It is a truth universally acknowledged, that a single man in possession of a good fortune, must be in want of a wife. However little known the feelings or views of such a man may be on his first entering a neighbourhood, this truth is so well fixed in the minds of the surrounding families that he is considered as the rightful property of some one or other of their daughters. | It is a truth universally acknowledged, that a single man in possession of a good fortune, must be in want of a wife. However little known the feelings or views of such a man may be on his first entering a neighbourhood, this truth is so well fixed in the minds of the surrounding families that he is considered as the rightful property of some one or other of their daughters. |

- Distinguish between **accents and apostrophes**. Accents are used to mark pronunciation in foreign words used in English, such as "café". Apostrophes mark the genitive of nouns ("the expert's opinion") or the omission of letters ("don't"). Do not mix them up.
- **Quotations** shorter than a) MLA7: three lines or b) MLA8: three lines of verse or four lines of prose are integrated

---

[7] Recent studies, however, claim that the presence or absence of serifs is not the only factor to be considered for readability. *Cf*. Aries Arditi and Jianna Cho, "Serifs and Font Legibility". *Vision Research* 45.23 (2005): 2926-2933. Web. 15 August 2019. <https://doi.org/10.1016/j.visres.2005.06.013>.

[8] Justification is a technical term in typesetting, meaning that the spaces between words or letters are stretched or compressed to create a block of text aligned to both margins.

into the text in double quotation marks (full stops, commas and semicolons should be after the author-page indication of the source in brackets). Longer quotations should be indented by 0.5 inch (1 cm) from the left margin without quotation marks (this is called a block quote). In MLA format, double spacing and font size are maintained. Some universities have style sheets demanding that block quotes be single-spaced in a font size slightly smaller than the regular text, with indentations from both the left and the right margin.

- **New paragraphs** should be indented by 0.5 inch (1 cm) from the left margin except for the first paragraph on a new page or after a block quote.
- **Underlining** is regarded as a relic from the days of mechanical typewriters. It is no longer used in the digital age. Headlines should be in bold face (maintaining the font size of the regular text).
- There are strict rules for **italics**. Use them for the titles of works that are not part of a larger work, such as books (*Frankenstein, or The Modern Prometheus*) or foreign words (*lege artis, ex cathedra*). If you use a scribal abbreviation for a title you would normally italicize (such as *NA* für *Northanger Abbey*), remember to italicize the abbreviation as well.
- The distinction between 'larger works' and 'smaller works' is not only required for your list of works cited, but for your whole paper! When you italicize *Hamlet*, you are talking about the **drama**. When you do not italicize Hamlet, you are talking about the **character**.
- **Do not use logos, colours, images, or graphic elements** unless they are absolutely necessary for your line of argument (such as stills when comparing a book with its film adaptation). If your word processing programme automatically formats hyperlinks in blue and underlined, turn off that function or manually remove the link.

- **Stick to the layout of the style sheet.** Do not leave out whole pages, nor start a new page with each chapter. Do not change the margins or the font size. Changing the format will not prevent you from having to meet the page limit. 10-12 pages according to the regulations stated here will result in 1400-5100 words in any format you choose – using a bigger font, wider margins and leaving out pages will do nothing but annoy your supervisor, who will probably request an electronic version of your paper for a word count.
- **Number your pages** in the upper right-hand corner (omit the number on the title page – start with the Table of Contents as page 2). **Use the same font type and size for page numbers** as for the rest of your paper.
- The **bibliography** is part of your Table of Contents, but as it is not a chapter of your paper, it does not have a number. Unless you are writing a PhD dissertation, there is no need to distinguish between primary and secondary literature in your paper. Note that the **affidavit** is not listed in the Table of Contents at all.
- **Do not use** contractions such as "don't", "haven't", 'won't". They are not normally used in written English. Avoid colloquialisms such as "gonna" or "stuff". Avoid starting sentences with "And" or "But".
- Distinguish hyphens (-) from dashes (–). Dashes are longer than hyphens. Hyphens are used to join compound words such as "user-friendly". Dashes indicate a break in the sentence: "This going off after luncheon for a walk, though Andrew was with them – what could it mean?"[9]

On proofreading your manuscript (you may ask someone else to do this, as you tend to overlook errors in a text you have written yourself), look out for ellipses (incomplete sentences), word repetitions, typos/spelling errors, and words hyphen-

---

[9]    Virginia Woolf, *To the Lighthouse* (Oxford: OUP, 2008), 47.

ated in the wrong place. There are options for automatic hyphenation and spell checkers in word processing software, however, there are contexts in which errors cannot be identified automatically, such as: "*Jaws* is a film about a man eating shark", as opposed to "*Jaws* is a film about a man-eating shark".[10] In this case, the hyphen alters the meaning of the sentence. In the first case, the film is about a man who is eating shark meat. As both varieties are sensible sentences, your word processing programme has no way of identifying this as an error.

Your final manuscript should not contain any typesetting errors such as widows and orphans, *i.e.* single lines separated from the rest of a paragraph by a page-break. A widow is a single line at the bottom of a page, an orphan is a single line at the top of a page.[11] Insert a manual page break or activate *Para WidowOrphanControl* in your software.

At most universities, the submission of a printed manuscript which contains a signed affidavit is still standard procedure. An electronic version of your paper as a PDF file may also be required, especially if your university uses plagiarism detection tools. Submitting your paper by e-mail is not an option without your supervisor's consent.

Print on one side of the paper only. You should hand in a spiral-bound manuscript or a clip folder. Please do not use page protectors. Imagine your supervisors correcting thirty seminar papers of twelve pages each; they would have to take a sheet from a page protector 360 times (and insert the sheets again afterwards). If they manage not to cut their fingers in

---

[10]    For more examples, see Lauren Hale, "9 Sentences That Need a Hyphen". *Ragan Communications*. Web. 17 August 2019. <https://www.ragan.com/9-sentences-that-need-a-hyphen/>.

[11]    Definitions may vary. The current *MLA Handbook* does not explicitly forbid widows and orphans, whereas the *Chicago Manual of Style* advises users to avoid them.

the process, they had still rather spend the time more effectively on giving you advice on your writing.

## Exercises

### Exercise 9.1: Language and Style
Identify and correct all errors in the following sentences. There may be more than one error in each sentence.

a) The murder of Duncan – which was the idea of Macbeth's wife – is a serious crime.
b) *Macbeth* believes he won't have to justify himself. But he is wrong.
c) In my first e-mail, I had forgotten the attachment, but I resent it.
d) You think you know everything about punctuation - but is that really true?

### Exercise 9.2: Works Cited
Prepare a list of works cited in MLA style. Research all bibliographic data required, arrange your entries in alphabetical order, and format them according to the recommendations of the MLA. Your bibliography should contain the following sources:

- Linda Hutcheon's famous book on the poetics of postmodernism
- The transcript of Barack Obama's inaugural address in 2009 from the ABC News website
- Valerie Rumbold's contribution on Pope and Gender in a companion to Alexander Pope issued by Cambridge University Press
- Lorraine Daston's article about curiosity in early modern science, published in an academic journal in 1995

- The DVD version of the episode "The Swords of Wayland Part 2" of a British TV series produced in the 1980s, set in Sherwood Forest, starring Michael Praed as Robin Hood.

# Chapter 10: Inventing Meatballs: Plagiarism

Ever since several prominent politicians were charged with plagiarism for their questionable practice of citation, it has been common knowledge that claiming other people's work as your own can have severe consequences.[1]

Today the concept of plagiarism seems to be much more present in the media and in public discussion than it was ten years ago. Reactions cover the entire spectrum from trivialization to bureaucratic regulatory frenzy. Just as varied as the opinions expressed are the causes of plagiarism. Psychological factors such as pressure from public authorities, employers or grant providers play a role here, as do poor time management, lack of familiarity with citation practice, or culturally different attitudes to the concept of intellectual property.[2] Studies on plagiarism have explored the impact of "gender, social circumstances, efficiency gain, motivation for study, methodological uncertainties or easy access to electronic information via the Internet and new technologies".[3]

Simplified access to electronic texts also means, however, that plagiarism is not only easier to produce today, but also more easily identified than ever before. Suspicious or familiar-

---

[1]  In 2011, German defence secretary Karl Theodor zu Guttenberg resigned his post after the University of Bayreuth revoked his doctoral degree. Not only did his transgression end his political career (at least for the time being), but it also made him the target of irony and satire, earning him nicknames such as "Baron zu Googleberg" and "the Secretary for Cut and Paste". Farida Fawzy, "From Speeches to PhDs: Politicians Called Out for Copying". *CNN Politics*. Web. 19 August 2019. <https://edition.cnn.com/2016/07/19/politics/politicians-plagiarism/index.html>.

[2]  On the problem of understanding intellectual property in different cultures *cf.* Darsie Bowden, "Stolen Voices: Plagiarism and Authentic Voice". *Composition Studies/Freshman English News* 24.1-2 (1996): 5-18.

[3]  Eva Jereb *e.a.*,"Factors Influencing Plagiarism in Higher Education: A comparison of German and Slovene Students". *PLoS One* 13.8 (2018). Web. 19 August 2019. <https://dx.doi.org/10.1371%2Fjournal.pone.0202252>.

looking phrases can be assigned to a source with the help of a search engine. There is also specialized software which automatically searches the internet as well as articles from databases and compares them with the work submitted. There are controversial debates among institutions as to whether the use of such programmes and the resulting compulsion to electronically submit assignments to universities is justified, especially since the existing software solutions to date may "yield quite modest results".[4] Does the demand for electronic "plagiarism hunter software" place all students under general suspicion, which is, in most cases, unjustified?

Does it then already constitute general suspicion to place students at individual tables in exams, to ask them to produce an ID card, or to prohibit the use of mobile phones during the examination? Most regulations contain such clauses without anyone feeling the need to discuss them at all. The balance has to be maintained: on the one hand to build trust between teachers and students, on the other hand to ensure that students who do not cheat are not effectively disadvantaged because of a few "black sheep". The socialisation of young researchers, which is indispensable for establishing common values within the scientific community, cannot succeed if a feeling of injustice or even indifference arises.[5]

Regardless of how individual institutions deal with cases of plagiarism, the fact remains that, despite a majority of students who adhere to good scientific practice, plagiarism occurs again and again in everyday university life.

---

[4]   Debora Weber-Wulff, Gabriele Wohnsdorf, "Strategien der Plagiatsbekämpfung", *Information Wissenschaft & Praxis*, Schwerpunkt "Plagiate und unethische Autorenschaften", 2 (2006), 90–98; 90. Weber-Wulff and Wohnsdorf tested various software solutions with ten sample essays, seven of which were the result of plagiarism, which had to be identified by the programs.

[5]   On the social acceptance of Illicit aids *cf*. Michael Josephson, "Willful Blindness about Cheating". *Student Cheating and Plagiarism in the Internet Era. A Wakeup Call*. Ed. Ann Lathrop and Kathleen Foss (Englewood, CO: Libraries Unlimited, 2000), 63.

John L. Waltman distinguishes deliberate plagiarism, "the wholesale copying of another's paper with the intention of representing it as one's own",[6] from unintentional plagiarism, "careless paraphrasing and citing of source material such that improper or misleading credit is given".[7] Basically, authors are guilty of plagiarism if they pass off someone else's ideas as their own, or if they fail to prevent those ideas from being taken for their own. According to this definition by Waltman, plagiarism does not have to mean that one has deliberately copied someone's thoughts and passed them off as one's own, it can also happen unintentionally, *e.g.* in the form of misleading paraphrases.[8]

Causes of involuntary plagiarism are insufficient research skills, imprecise management of notes, and confusion about citation systems.[9] According to a US study, up to 60% of students cannot distinguish between plagiarism and paraphrase.[10]

Failing to provide the bibliographical record of one single quotation may formally suffice to be charged with plagiarism. Since it is impossible to prove an intention to deceive beyond doubt, the work can be rejected on this basis alone. How much 'inspiration' is acceptable, what does one not have to prove at all, and how are other people's ideas to be formally marked? How do you evade stress and careless note-taking? Once you have worked through this chapter, you should be able to avoid involuntary plagiarism in your writing.

---

[6]   John L. Waltman, "Plagiarism: Preventing it in Formal Research Papers". *ABCA Bulletin* 43.2 (1980): 37-8, 37.

[7]   *Ibid*.

[8]   On the controversy over the deliberate intention to deceive as the sole criterion for cases of plagiarism *cf*. Weber-Wulff und Wohnsdorf, "Strategien der Plagiatsbekämpfung", 90.

[9]   Anna Bombak, "Guide to Plagiarism and Cyberplagiarism". University of Alberta. 13 July 2010. < http://guides.library.ualberta.ca/content.php?pid=62200 &sid=3013167>.

[10]  *Ibid*. The quoted study is by Miguel Roig, "When College Students' Attempts at Paraphrasing Become Instances of Potential Plagiarism". *Psychological Reports* 84 (1999): 973-82, 914.

## 10.1 How to Invent Meatballs: Giving Credit

The good news is that you do not have to give credit for every bit of information that you received from someone else. There are certain basic terms that at least the vast majority of your readers should be aware of and/or whose authors can no longer be identified. The writer Angela Carter explained, for example, that the origins of the fairy tales she used as the basis for her short stories were just as difficult to document as it was to identify the inventor of meatballs without any doubt.[11] Accordingly, you do not need to look for evidence of who introduced the stock character of the witch into the fairy tale tradition, or document the fact that the witches are evil in most fairy tales. If you refer to the witch from Hansel and Gretel however, you should have a source and document it so that your readers know whether you mean the Brothers Grimm or the Ludwig Bechstein version.

### General Knowledge

According to the Viennese educationalist Richard Olechowski, the general knowledge so frequently invoked in the public discussion is "the acquisition of basic competences in as many areas of life as possible for the critical examination of the entire physical and spiritual reality of life".[12]

General knowledge may originate in all walks of life; it is knowledge that is both known to many people and not subject-specific. The fact that the earth revolves around the sun

---

[11]   Angela Carter in Dani Cavallaro, *The World of Angela Carter: A Critical Investigation* (Jefferson, NC: McFarland, 2011), 17.

[12]   Richard Olechowski, "Allgemeinbildung". *Institut für Erziehungswissenschaft Universität Wien.* 09 April 2013.
<http://homepage.univie.ac.at/richard.olechowski/statements/allgemeinbildung.html>.

or that George Washington was the first President of the USA no longer needs to be scientifically proven. Proverbs such as "You can lead a horse to water, but you can't make it drink" can no longer be traced back to an author and are regarded as general knowledge. As soon as one makes a statement about which there are divided opinions, which constitutes an interpretation, it must be substantiated.

**Example:**

> Margaret Thatcher was Britain's first woman Prime Minister.

General knowledge, no credit required.

> In spite of being Britain's first woman Prime Minister, Margaret Thatcher was often criticized for failing to advance the political cause of feminism (*cf.* Evans 25).

No general knowledge, documentation/credit required. The statement represents one possible interpretation of Thatcher's political work and is discussed in detail in the literature cited.[13]


**Basic knowledge of the subject**

As already mentioned, you may assume that the target audience of your paper is an interested peer group. This means that you do not have to explain or document the basics of your subject, such as those taught in the introductory course. You may assume that your readers know what a metaphor is, or that poetry is a major literary genre. No evidence is required. If, however, you are concerned with the subtleties of a term, such as satirical writing by Jonathan Swift, you should first clarify some of the basics of the term satire, describe how you would like to use it, and, of course, substantiate this definition.

---

[13]   Eric Evans, *Thatcher and Thatcherism. The Making of the Contemporary World* (London: Routledge, ²2004), 25.

## Knowledge from the course, course materials, handouts by fellow students

Usually you conclude a seminar you have attended with a written term paper. Since the topics of the paper are aligned to the skills you are supposed to acquire, it is obvious that you want to show that you have understood the contents of the seminar, and that you are able to reproduce and transfer them in your own work. Nevertheless, you cannot use knowledge from the course like subject-specific basic knowledge. Even situations you have worked with every week in the course and which you are now taking for granted remain someone else's ideas and must be identified as such.

It is not sufficient to quote the slides of your lecturers, which may have been posted on an e-learning platform, as a source. These materials are created for a completely different purpose – they should make it easier for you to understand the contents of the course and serve as a reminder. Therefore, the didactic content of the courses is very different from that of a scientific article on the same topic in a professional journal. Often facts are simplified or reduced to the aspects relevant to the learning outcome. The course material is therefore not suitable for quoting! Take a close look at the documents. Have your lecturers added references at the end of the slide series? Can you access to these sources via the library or the internet? Do not hesitate to ask if in doubt. The same applies to handouts that you have received from your fellow students after a presentation.

## Public Domain – available to all, but no *carte blanche*

If a text, image or programme is marked as public domain, this means that anyone may use the material unaltered with reference to the original source, free of charge. You can take a photo of your dog with your mobile phone, upload this photo as an example of "Golden Retriever" to an online encyclopaedia and specify: the image should be public domain. This means that everyone is allowed to use this picture, the primary school pupil who gives a presentation on Golden Retrievers as well as the professional dog trainer who is currently writing a book about the behaviour of a Golden Retriever. Both have to indicate you as the picture source. You do not earn anything from it and you cannot sue for a profit share if the book becomes a bestseller thanks to your dog picture on the cover (as long as the dog trainer does not claim to have shot the picture himself, because that would infringe on your rights as owner). A work can become public domain not only by explicit declaration, but also in other ways.

If the author of a novel died at least 70 years ago, his text automatically becomes public domain in many countries.[14] This does not mean, however, that you can download Shakespeare's *Othello* from the Internet (*e.g.* from Project Gutenberg), throw away the title page and attach a new one to it, *Othello, or I had a really bad day – A drama by Jane Doe*. It just means: If Jane Doe enjoys offering the Project Gutenberg script of *Othello* for free download on her website or wants to quote from it, then she can do so and does not have to be concerned about anyone charging for it. So Public Domain only clarifies the rights of use, intellectual property remains unaffected! *Othello* remains Shakespeare's *Othello* (if Shakespeare really was the author – but this is a completely different problem).

---

[14]    Copyright regulations vary among different countries and can be very complex. Please check individual copyright laws in your country of residence.

## 10.2 Strategies to Avoid Unintentional Plagiarism

Unintentional plagiarism is mostly caused by careless documentation during the research process. The time it takes to complete a paper is usually limited by examination regulations, so there is no room for negotiation, if one week prior to the deadline, you still have only a few pages to offer. With poor time management skills, you'll be under pressure more quickly and be tempted to stop documenting your sources carefully. This problem can easily be solved, however, without risking expulsion.

### Strategy 1: Use your time wisely.

If there are still so many blank pages left close to the deadline, this is mostly due to the fact that, especially at the beginning of your studies, you have little experience of how long it takes to write a paper or to prepare the manuscript, and what amount of extra work you can do in the same period of time without this being at the expense of your term paper. Therefore, when setting up your timetable, pay attention to which courses will require you to write a term paper in the end and how many semesters you have left to complete these courses. **Keep your workload manageable!** It is better to attend only one seminar per semester which finishes with a term paper than trying to produce five papers at once.

**Start the preparatory work in good time.** Try to find a topic and suitable literature while the course is still running. When registering for a presentation in the course, consider whether the topic is suitable for expanding it into a term paper. If you are already familiar with the topic at the beginning of the writing process because you have already done some research and and presented some key points in class, this will reduce the amount of research to be carried out for the final paper.

**Set priorities.** Plan your vacation so that you will not have to take your books to the beach (you will not do that very often, anyway).

### Strategy 2: Look for support offered by your university.

Your writing process is much more efficient if you talk to the lecturer time and time again to address open questions. Do not be too shy to ask. Nobody will judge you because you admit that you did not understand everything about the topic, or that you are having trouble with an article from secondary literature. On the contrary: a few specific questions show that you have dealt with your topic intensely. Of course, in return, you are also expected to have 'done your homework' beforehand. Independent research is part of your assessment. Draw up a list with all ambiguities and questions before you go to the office hour. Write an abstract on your topic, show your supervisors a Table of Contents or a selected bibliography. This way, errors in structuring, misunderstandings regarding the topic, or unsuitable secondary literature can be detected at an early stage.

Ideally, you should see your lecturers in their office hours three times: at the beginning of your work, to find a topic and roughly determine the direction it might take; after the research phase, when you have already formed a concrete idea of your work and have gathered some material; and after assessment. In an individual interview you will learn where you have scored in your paper and which aspects you should still work on.

The support offered, however, does not only include the supervision of your writing process by the lecturer. Word processing courses, writing workshops, time management courses, and coaching are offered by many universities, often by computer centres or equal opportunities officers. In Germany, a lot of universities also take part in the "Long Night of

Postponed Papers". Every first Thursday of March, the participating institutions provide their students with professional help for writing projects to come to a good conclusion at last. Writing counselling, workshops, motivational training and relaxation exercises are all part of the programme.[15] While writing papers is usually a rather lonesome process with few opportunities for exchange, the Long Night impressively demonstrates that you are not alone after all.

### Strategy 3: Be persuasive of yourself.

Why did you actually come to the university? Because you want a nice certificate to hang on your wall? Or because you want to acquire the knowledge and skills you will need in your future profession? In a scientific paper you should learn to acquire knowledge of a topic at your own initiative and to present this in an appealing and convincing way.

If you choose the profession of a teacher, you will need these skills every day. The class will notice relatively quickly if you are knowledgeable in your field and if you can teach it. Think back to the trainees you experienced during your school days. Surely after a very short time you were already aware of which of them were actually suitable candidates to be teachers. If you prefer to work in economy, the ability to build a structured argument will help you convince others – at first to hire you instead of the other 100 applicants, then to realize your ideas and projects.

---

[15]    A list of the participating institutions with programmes can be found at <http://schreibnacht.wordpress.com/>.

## Strategy 4: Document your sources.

Documenting your sources begins with such a trivial process as photocopying a chapter from a book. Copy not only the relevant chapter, but also the title page and imprint. This way, you already have all the information you need for your list of works cited. Even if you do not make any photocopies and only write an abstract about a source, take down the exact page number for each individual thought. Nothing is more annoying than having to borrow a book again because you missed out on the page number of an important quotation in the first place. Print out the internet pages you want to use and note the author, title of the page, and institution. You can set your browser so that the Internet address (URL) and the date of access also appear on the printout.

## Exercises

### Exercise 10: Avoiding Plagiarism
Do the following cases constitute plagiarism? (give reasons)

a) Someone downloads a term paper from an internet page, adds a new title page to it, and submits it as his own.
b) Someone asks his girlfriend to proofread his paper and check for typos.
c) Someone uses the thesaurus function of his word processing programme.
d) Someone uses the term 'symbol' without defining it.
e) Someone writes down the interpretation of a drama scene jointly developed in the course and uses it in his term paper.
f) Someone quotes the interpretation of a scene from an academic essay and mentions the source in MLA style once at the end of the chapter.

g) Someone reproduces the content of an article in their own words and indicates the article in the bibliography.

h) Someone reflects thoughts about a novel from a customer review of an internet bookseller in his work.

# Chapter 11: Strategies for Exams

You have just spent considerable time reflecting on research papers and oral exams; written exams are nonetheless still the most common form of assessment in many countries. Although you have already passed a lot of written exams in school, you will notice some differences to this type of assessment at university. First and foremost, you do not normally take more than one written exam in a course, meaning that the final test covers the content of a whole semester. If you were used to studying only the night before the test when you were in school, this strategy will not be helpful at university.

Whereas a lot of exam questions you answered in school could be managed with a strategy which is, though politically incorrect, frequently referred to as 'bulimic learning' (learning a lot of facts by heart, regurgitating them during the exam and then forgetting about them), exams at university follow the strategy of constructive alignment; that means you are supposed to demonstrate in your exam that you have acquired a set of skills you are going to need in your job. Prepare for exams in a way that you will remember the content of the course later, not only for the exam.

It is therefore sensible to revise the content of the course each week, by typing or neatly rewriting your notes and adding to them by extra reading. Your revision will be much easier, and you will be able to see the focal points of the course more clearly. Revising in a study group and comparing each other's notes may also help you cover a large amount of content, especially in literary theory, terminology, or history.

Preparation for the exam starts before the first course meeting. When reading your primary texts, which you should ideally have already finished before you enter the classroom for the first time, mark important passages and take notes, especially on the plot and characters. This way, you do not need to spend valuable time on re-reading the primary texts before the exam because after six months of study you cannot remember the details. Learn to spell names and places correctly – show that you are aware of the difference between (Ben) Jonson, Shakespeare's contemporary, and (Samuel) Johnson, the eighteenth-century polymath. If you attend a seminar on a particular genre or literary period, read up on it. No one expects you to be an expert on Restoration comedy before the course has even started, but it would be nice to know who or what was restored, and if that happened in the seventeenth or twentieth century. In an advanced seminar on literary theory, the lecturer would expect you to have some knowledge of the introductory course. If you cannot remember how to tell a metaphor from metonymy, browse through your notes from the introductory course. Terminology can be studied like vocabulary, using index cards you can easily divide into stacks. Whenever you come across a new theoretical term, write an index card (term on the one side, definition and example on the other). Revise from time to time. You can also use different colours for different fields, e.g. yellow for stylistic devices, green for poetry, blue for drama, etc.

Whereas careful preparation of exams is a success factor, it is by no means the only one. Being well-informed about the form and duration of the exam, the grading system, and exam regulations may prevent unpleasant surprises. You can usually download exam regulations from your university website. Legally, the only binding version is the printed form at the registrar's or examination office. Furthermore, you can significantly improve your exam results if you take a moment to read questions carefully and consider your strategy for the questions in front of you.

**Can you read?**
This may sound like a trivial question, downright insulting if you study English or American literature, however, reading in this case means understanding the demands of a questions.

## 11.1 Types of Questions in Written Exams

The type of question already determines the structure of the answer! Basically, exam questions fall into three categories: reproducing what you have read or learnt by heart, transferring what you know onto different situations and contexts, and solving more complex problems, applying in practice what you have learnt. Questions of the first category are usually awarded the least amount of credit (devote less time to those questions and write only a little text here), whereas problem-solving questions will earn you the most credit (as these questions are the most demanding, a higher degree of reflection and abstraction is required, so reserve enough time for those questions). Here are a few keywords to help you analyse exam instructions:[1]

**Reproducing knowledge:**

- **State:** Provide terminology here, list the most important aspects. No further explanations or details are required.
- **Define:** Give the meaning of the term, as precisely as possible. Definitions may vary in terms of context and author.
- **Outline:** Summarize briefly and precisely.

---

[1]    Many universities offer lists and guidelines on essay and exam questions on their websites. Particularly elaborate lists of instruction words can be found at "Instruction Verbs in Essay Questions". *University of Kent at Canterbury.* Web. 29 September 2019. <https://www.kent.ac.uk/ai/ask/documents/step_1_Instruction_verbs.pdf>, and "Essay Terms Explained". *University of Leicester.* Web. 29 September 2019. <https://www2.le.ac.uk/offices/ld/resources/writing/writing-resources/essay-terms>.

**Knowledge transfer:**

- **Explain:** A mere list of technical terms is not enough, you will need to clarify what is meant by it.
- **Describe:** Provide the typical features of a character or the individual steps of a process.
- **Illustrate:** Give evidence from the text, examples, facts. Show why the thesis applies or does not apply. The question must be related to concrete aspects of the chosen text. A theoretical essay without reference to a text is not sufficient.
- **Compare**: Identify mainly similarities, for example between two literary theories, periods, characters.
- **Contrast:** Identify mainly differences.

**Solving a problem:**

- **Analyse:** Take the text apart and critically evaluate each subtopic or aspect.
- **Discuss:** Look at the question/problem from different angles, general answers are unfavourable, weigh pros and cons, draw conclusions.
- **Assess:** Weigh different arguments and judge whether a thesis or claim is justified.

Think strategically when calculating the amount of time you have to answer those questions. When the exam starts, consider how much time in total there is, how many questions you have to answer, and how much each question is 'worth' in terms of credit. Spend more time on questions which are likely to gain you a lot of credit, such as essay questions starting with "Analyse", "Discuss", or "Assess". Is the question divided into several parts? If so, make sure you answer each of them and double check that you have considered them all towards the end of the exam. Do not waste a lot of time on "define" or single/multiple choice questions. It is ok to start with an easy question, however, you should not let your quest for the perfect phrasing of a simple definition stop you from moving on to the scary essay question that will make up 30% of the grade.

**Single and multiple choice questions.** Most of these questions belong to the first category, requiring mere reproduction of knowledge. They consist of the so-called stem, which is the question or problem, and several alternatives to choose from.

In **single choice** questions, only one answer is correct. The remaining alternatives are there to distract you, so the best way of approaching such a question is not to look at them at first.

In a good SC/MC question, all important information is contained in the stem. Cover the alternatives with your hand and ask yourself: what would your answer be if there were no alternatives? Make up your mind before looking at the alternatives.

If you have no idea what the question is all about, do not leave out any single choice questions; a good guess is better than no answer at all. Most single choice questions with three to five options can be narrowed down to two answers with a little common sense. As it is quite difficult to think of three alternatives which are equally plausible, one of the answers often is complete nonsense, one of them is a distractor from the depths of the brain of your lecturer and probably refers to something you have never heard of (which nevertheless works as a distractor), and one of them is as plausible as the best solution. If you manage to eliminate nonsense and far-fetched alternatives, that leaves you with a 50% chance of hitting the correct answer.

**Multiple choice questions** are trickier because you never know how many answers are correct. Wrong or missing answers are usually penalized, which is why you have to narrow down your choices even if you need to guess because you do not know the correct answer. Again, first of all, eliminate nonsense and far-fetched alternatives. Carefully evaluate each remaining alternative. There are two myths concerning multiple choice tests which are still spread on the Internet: "The longest answer is always the correct one", and "c) is always correct". In a good MC test, all answers have the same length, and the answers are mixed up at random. Some sites will also advise you to skip questions you cannot answer right away – personally, I think that one multiple choice question worth 2 or 3 credits out of 100 is not worth the trouble, as most students forget they left it out. Answering all questions in the given order "consulting your own sense of the probable", as Jane Austen's Henry Tilney would say, seems to me the better alternative. If you do decide to skip a question because you are momentarily confused by alternatives that seem too similar, mark the question (highlighter, question mark at the margin of the page) to make sure you will remember addressing it later.

## 11.2 Exams: DOs and DON'Ts

### DON'Ts

### 1. Do not use bullet points.

Without any complete sentences, a text lacks necessary coherence. It is impossible for the corrector to know whether you are aware of what each bullet point means in detail. You may have just recalled a term you heard in class without being able to relate it to the question. Take up buzz words from the question. Imagine a question such as: "Identify the narrative perspective of the text and describe its characteristics".

Answers such as

- autodiegetic (Genette)
- internal focalization
- high potential of identification
- but: unreliability

are unfortunately not very helpful. Write in complete sentences. Compare the bullet points to the following answer: "According to Genette, the text is written in an autodiegetic voice, which means the person speaking is also the protagonist of the story. The text uses internal focalization, as the thoughts conveyed are only those of the narrator; the reader knows what the character in the story knows, nothing more. Characteristically, autodiegetic texts help readers to identify with the character, as there is no mediating narrator between the reader and the character. There is, however, the question of reliability; as the narrator's point of view is limited, he or she may not be aware of all the facts, or may be lying for some hidden purpose."

You should always add "flesh to the bones", the mere framework of an answer can hardly be assessed at all.

2. **Do not weaken your own answers with empty phrases!** If the idea is wrong, your uncertainty will not save your exam grade. If the idea is right, the uncertainty will reduce the impression of the answer to a "chance hit". Answers such as "It seems to be an autodiegetic narrator" should therefore be avoided. Better: "The fact that the narrator himself is the protagonist of the events he describes means that this is an autodiegetic text".

3. **Do not use brackets** in your text except for page or line numbers; in all other contexts, use dashes or commas to separate one part of the sentence from another.

4. **Do not** take too many notes. What you write on scribbling paper is, in most exams, only for yourself and may not be graded. If your exam consists only of essay questions, no

more than one third of the time available should be used on note-taking and drafting.

5. **Do not copy** someone else's answers. The goal of an exam is not to receive a grade, but to test your knowledge and skills, which you are going to need in your career. If your learning outcome is zero, you will be harming yourself even if you get away with it.


## DOs

1. **Use technical terms!!!** Even if an answer is correct in terms of content, a missing technical term will lose you points. As in any other academic discipline, the safe use of terminology is part of the "tools of the trade". Those who have difficulties in clearly defining terms should clarify the "cases of doubt" in the library by means of corresponding reference books and familiarise themselves with them as quickly as possible. *A Glossary of Literary Terms* will help you close any gaps.

2. If there is a text you work with, **copy quotations correctly**! Copying errors leave a bad impression and can easily be avoided.

3. **Always quote from the text**. There is a reason, after all, that the text is there. If the lecturer had wanted an abstract treatise, he would not have provided a text.

4. **Read your own answer critically at the end!!! Avoid obvious contradictions!**
   Examples (not recommended for imitation): "The narrator is autodiegetic. He has a limited point of view of the world he has created."
   
   An autodiegetic narrator is the protagonist of his story, in other words part of the world he depicts. Being all-powerful is characteristic of the heterodiegetic (Stanzel: authorial) narrative perspective. The answer thus contains

an obvious contradiction – if the narrator. is the one who created the world of the story, how could his point of view be limited?

5. **Make an effort for academic style and register**. The time you have in an exam is limited, however, avoiding colloquial language and using terminology is part of the qualification you are trying to achieve.

## 11.3 Strategies for Essay Questions

The type of question most credits are awarded for is usually the essay question. You receive a text or an extract from a text, as well as a few questions. It is your task to answer these questions in the form of an essay, tackling each question either separately, or as a coherent text. As you are not writing your essay at home, you are not expected to quote from secondary literature, but you are often expected to refer to well-known stances in reception, hermeneutics, and literary theory as background knowledge. The advantage of this type of question is that you can refer to a concrete text, find hints in the text as to what is required in the task. If you know the text, you can score points by demonstrating your knowledge of the context. That does not imply you are at a disadvantage if you have not read the text, or if it is a relatively unknown text by a well-known author. Try to establish links to what you already know. In this case, transfer is required. There may be other texts by the same author that you have read, or other texts of the same time frame you are more familiar with which share the same themes or narrative techniques.

A good strategy to approach an unfamiliar text is situating it within the context of literary history. What important events occurred immediately before the text (*e.g.* French Revolution, World Wars)? What political, philosophical, historical, literary, cultural influences affect this text? Do you recognize the influence of literary predecessors or role-models (such as antiquity)? What effects does this text have on its literary successors? Does it do pioneer work? Is there a tradition it adopts or rejects? You do not need to write a long introduction as in your research paper at home, two or three paragraphs providing some context is enough.

You may also use your knowledge of the author (*e.g.* atheist, feminist, deserter, suicide ..). The modernist poet William Butler Yeats lived close by the post office in Dublin, which became the site of the Irish Easter Rising in 1916. Interpreting Yeats' poem "Easter 1916" is quite difficult without any knowledge of Yeats' biography and his attitude towards the independence movement. Be aware, however, that you cannot base your entire interpretation on the biography and disregard everything else. Since the New Criticism of Wimsatt and Beardsley, modern literary theory rejects standard interpretations based on the life of an author. It is considered "biographical fallacy" to assume that a poet's views are identical to the opinion expressed by the speaker of a poem, or that the events occurring in a novel really happened to its author. Postmodern critics such as Roland Barthes even insist that the author has no part in determining the meaning of his or her text ("The Death of the Author"). As long as you show that you are aware of the difficulty biographical norms of interpretation can generate, you are on the safe side.

Closely related to the historical situation is the question of literary tradition. It is easier to place a text within a certain tradition if you look at the genre or form and the themes addressed in the text. Which "big issues" are covered (e.g. love, death, religion, ethics, nature, alterity/racism/colonialism, class, society/social issues, violence, education, youth, age)?

What is the attitude of the speaker and/or other characters towards these issues? A Romantic may idealize nature, a Victorian may believe in progress, a Modernist may feel estranged from both – avoid reducing a literary period to such clichés though, always check for clues in the text. The more you differentiate and look at ideas from different perspectives, the better.

## 11.4 Sample Analysis

### W.H. Auden, "If I Could Tell You" (written in 1940)

Working time: 180 minutes

The primary text for this analysis can be found in W.H. Auden, "If I Could Tell You". *Collected Poems*. Ed. Edward Mendelson. New York: Random House/Vintage, 1991, 314. It is one of Auden's most frequently quoted poems.

1. Describe the situation of the lyrical I with special emphasis on the depiction of time.
2. Analyse the poem in terms of structural characteristics, language, and style.
3. Situate the poem in the context of its origin. Refer to another poetic text written after 1900 with similar thematic orientation.

Step 1: Read the poem. Mark anything that strikes you as unusual. Write down keywords for associations you have with the text (Time? Author? Genre? Themes?).

   Step 2: Read all the questions first. Ensure you understand what you are supposed to do. The verbs in the question will help (describe, analyse, situate, refer to).

Step 3: Read the poem again through the lens of the question. Use different colours to mark important parts in the text for different questions. Write on the margins of the text. Take notes on scribbling paper (bullet points, buzz words).

Step 4: Two thirds of the time available should be spent on the writing process. Start with a short introduction of 2-3 (meaningful, contextualizing) paragraphs, then head straight into the question.

**The following text will give you some hints as to how the questions can be answered. There are many different ways of approaching an essay question, so this is by no means the ultimate answer.**

### Question 1

W.H. Auden is a modernist poet. Modernist poetry is characterized by conflict between different notions of poetry, especially the classical understanding of the poet as a seer, or *vates*, as to be seen in the Movement, and the radical experiment of intellectual, elitist poetry of Eliot and Pound. One of the major discussions is the question of the involvement of poetry in society; whereas the War Poets of WWI showed a deep commitment to portraying the horrors of war, attacking romanticized, patriotic ideals of heroism, after WWII the question was raised whether poetry was able to accomplish anything in society at all.

Auden belongs to an influential generation of poets who found themselves in a world of social tensions, having barely recovered from the trauma of WWI. Among these Thirties Poets, he was so influential that the group of poets around him is referred to as the Auden Group (or MacSpaunday, being an acronym of the surnames of its members). By the time Auden wrote "If I Could Tell You", he had been deeply concerned with the topic of war. Having documented the Japanese-Chinese war in the 1930s, he had returned to the UK in 1938, with an imminent war in Europe.

The speaker of the poem shares his reflections on time. It is evident from the pessimistic tone of the poem that the speaker lives in difficult times which hardly provide any form of orientation, a topic typical of Modernism. Time is personified (see capitalization in l.18), but speaks only one sentence, "I told you so" (l.1). Therefore, developments in modern times are inevitable and predestined by anonymous forces, but for the individual they remain unfathomable ("If I could tell you, I would let you know", l. 3). The time in which the speaker lives is marked by uncertainties and fears, especially the fear of death, the "price" one pays for time ("Time only knows the price we have to pay", l. 2).

The paradoxical structures of the reality of the lyrical I become particularly clear in the second stanza through the juxtaposition of opposites: Clowns are supposed to make people (especially children) laugh (l. 4), in fact the lyrical I wonders whether crying would not be more appropriate. The innocent, carefree laughter of childhood is lost, music makes people stumble, not dance (l. 5). Through the memory of better times, the elegiac tone of the poem becomes clear: happiness can only be experienced as loss. The future is so uncertain that not even a fortune-teller would try to predict it ("There are no fortunes to be told", l. 7). Nevertheless, the text cannot be assigned to the subgenre of elegy alone, as it echoes love poetry. The haunting image of a dark, fateful future is followed by a thematic break in which the speaker declares his love for an unnamed counterpart, "Because I love you more than I can say" (l. 8). This love, however, is bound to silence, "If I could tell you I would let you know" (l. 9), the speaker does not want to or is unable to talk about his feelings.

A biographical interpretation should always be treated with caution; Wimsatt and Beardsley claim that the speaker of a poem is by no means to be equated with the poet/ writer and may not automatically be regarded as the mouthpiece for his or her sensitivities. Drawing conclusions based solely on Auden's biography would therefore have to be considered a case of biographical fallacy. The silence of the lyrical persona could, however, be interpreted as an allusion to a forbidden, homosexual relationship. Homosexuality was a crime in the UK until 1967, and even Lord Alfred Douglas, Oscar Wilde's lover, used inevitable secrecy as a code for homosexuality, "The love that dare not speak its name".[2] Auden, who was homosexual, immortalized Wilde's arrest in one of his poems. Thus, the silence imposed on the speaker about his love could indicate their illegality.

Possibly, the difficult times in which the lovers live simply leave no room for interpersonal relationships, since they are characterized by images of decay; the fourth line evokes a desolate autumn landscape. The search for the meaning of life – "The winds must come from somewhere" (l. 10), "There must be reason why the leaves decay" (l. 11) – is not answered, the passage of time is the only thing that is certain. The individual cannot recognize any causality or linear progress, since the leitmotif of "Time will say nothing but I told you so" points to a cyclic repetition of patterns which will inevitably come to pass.

The situation of the lyrical I is by no means hopeless. In the fifth line, the theme of decay is broken by using the rose as a traditional motif of love poetry. The Romantics regarded the rose as a symbol of love, confidence and beauty, for example John Keats.

Here the roses are personified and have their own will: "Perhaps the roses really want to grow" (l.13). The metaphor of autumn is disrupted by an image of spring, beauty and

---

[2]   The intertextual reference to Douglas is not necessary, but can serve contextualization to interpret the line in question as a reference to homosexuality.

growth, at the same time the rose symbolizes the feelings of the lyrical I for the other person, which are characterized as serious and of lasting interest (l.14). At the same time, the speaker characterizes these thoughts as a "vision" (l.14), which emphasizes the (still) unreal nature of love and the newly emerging life, while at the same time expressing the epiphany inherent in the idea: a positive vision of the future seems possible with the help of love, changing the lyrical persona's views of time. If it had previously appeared as inexorable fate, the passage of time is given a positive aspect in the last verse: "the brooks and soldiers run away" (l.17), as the river flows by, so time also flows, and the war will end sometime. The leitmotif has changed from an irrefutable fact to a question: "Will Time say nothing but I told you so?" Whether after the end of the war people will be able to realize the speaker's positive vision or will instead witness history repeating remains uncertain: "If I could tell you, I would let you know" (l.19).

## Question 2

Auden uses the Villanelle form for this poem, which is rare in modern poetry: 19 lines divided into 5 tercets and a quartet, with the rhyming scheme aba aba aba aba aba abaa abaa – and iambic pentameter as metre (such as Dylan Thomas' "Do Not Go Gentle into That Good Night"). Through the forceful musicality of this form, the structure of the poem reflects its content by imitating the cyclic repetition and the constant rhythmic passing of time. The Villanelle form, originally from the pastoral, also underlines the elegiac tone of the first four tercets; by using an old form that originally served to idealize nature, the loss of old values and landmarks becomes clear.

Two verses are repeated alternately at the end of each stanza: (1) "Time will say nothing but I told you so" (ll. 1, 6, 12) and (2) "If I could tell you, I would let you know" (ll. 3, 9, 15).

By using them as leitmotifs, the text showcases its two main themes; the cyclical repetition of past mistakes in the flow of time, and the speaker's uncertainty about a reliable assessment of his situation and options for action. While the motif of time is changed by the transformation into a question in l. 18 and displays hope and a way out of chaos, the uncertainty of the speaker remains.

The language of the poem is kept simple in the style of the Thirties Poets. In order to remain comprehensible to a mass audience, the mystical charging of the text with symbols and elitist use of language as code is avoided. The text nevertheless uses rhetorical schemata and tropes, which can also be functionalized according to the requirements of the analysis of language and style:

- Anaphora ll. 1,2: "Time .. Time": urgency, time is established as a motif.
- Personification ll. 1,2: "Time will say nothing", "Time only knows". Time is almost depicted as a goddess, omnipotent, relentless.
- Parallelism: ll. 4,5: "If we should weep.../ If we should stumble": reflects the eternal cylical repetition of the similar, man does not learn from his mistakes, therefore the only constants in his life are suffering and death.
- Metaphor: "why the leaves decay" (l. 11), motif of decline, dying nature and falling leaves in autumn represent human death.
- Symbol: "perhaps the roses really want to grow" – rose for love, beauty, confidence. "the lions" (l.16): Strength, courage, but also danger. Biblical allusion: On Judgment Day the lion lies peacefully at the side of the lamb.
- Zeugma: "the brooks and soldiers run away" (l.17), the stream flows, the soldiers run away ➜ two different levels of meaning of "run away" are combined. The more water flows down the stream, *i.e.* the more time passes, the more

pointless the war becomes, and the soldiers run away. In a way, however, there is hope that time is a healer.

## Question 3

Auden wrote the poem in 1940, a year after the outbreak of World War II. As a Thirties Poet, Auden belongs to a generation that had to experience both World Wars. Thus the strong emphasis on time, which is perceived as a mechanism of repetitions of old mistakes, reflects the war experience of his contemporaries. The speaker feels like a plaything of anonymous powers that has no influence on his future and experiences it as chaotic, contingent and characterized by entropy (possible point of comparison to Thomas Hardy's "Hap"). The individual is solipsistic and isolated, since he cannot express his feelings (possible point of comparison to T.S. Eliot's "The Lovesong of J. Alfred Prufrock"), traditional forms of love poetry – "roses" – are revealed as naive and offer no solution to the "pathology of communication" (Habermas).

All aspects of life are characterized by a common structure of decay, as expressed by the autumn motif. Reasons for events are not recognizable (ll. 10,11). Here a similarity to one of the key texts of modern literature, W.B. Yeat's "The Second Coming", opens up.

Yeats' poem also assumes that history runs in cycles, whereby the cycle of Christianity draws to an end after 2,000 years in order to clear the way for something threatening, violent, which Yeats depicts by the ambiguous symbol of a sphinx. While Yeats' text is interspersed with biblical and mythological motifs, rendering it difficult to read without a classical, humanistic education, Auden focusses on images that are comprehensible to a wide audience: the war is depicted as a lion, strong and courageous on the one hand, but dangerous and deadly on the other. Unlike Yeats' Sphinx, whose reign is just

beginning ("What rough beast / Slouching towards Bethle-
hem to be born?"), there is still hope in Auden's poem that
the lions or attackers will retreat with the passing of time.

All in all, towards the end, Auden's text appears more
conciliatory and less hopeless than Yeats' text, recurring to
the Biblical apocalypse. Both poems show impressively the
uprooting of the modern individual and the threats of a complex world dominated by violence, in which people fall back
on themselves and find no explanation in the "grand narratives". Auden' s text succeeds, however, in showing an opportunity to overcome the cycles of power, violence and death
with the help of love in the uncertainty of the future.

Note: Since Auden's poem was written in a war situation,
it would also be possible to compare it with a poem by the
War Poets, but the selection is difficult, since most (anti-)war
poems focus on the harsh reality at the front and less on the
*conditio humana*.

### 11.5 Oral Exams

Oral exams differ from written ones because you are face-to-
face with the examiner. Many students dread oral exams
because reactions have to be relatively spontaneous, the time
to think about a question is limited, you cannot normally skip
a question, and your being nervous tends to show more than
in a written exam. The good news is that your examiners also
experience at least some degree of 'stage fright' – they have
also prepared for the exam, trying to figure out the best questions for you, and they also prefer giving you a good grade
to seeing you fail. Try to think of the oral exam as an opportunity to take part in an expert discussion on a topic you have
prepared for.

When you enter the room, there are usually at least two
examiners. The second examiner may ask questions as well,

or only write the protocol. He or she may not even teach the same subject as your lecturer. Linguists protocol exams in literature or culture and vice versa. He or she will nonetheless have an impression of how the exam went, whether you answered questions fluently or hesitantly, whether you knew the answers by yourself or needed some help from your lecturer. It is quite probable that the second examiner will share these impressions with your lecturer, or that your lecturer consults the protocol before making up his or her mind about your grade. Therefore, take heed not only of what you answer, but also how.

Old-fashioned rules of politeness apply – do not enter the room until you are asked to, greet both examiners, do not offer a handshake yourself. It is always the older person who offers to shake hands, and especially during exam time in winter, many lecturers refrain from shaking hands for hygienic reasons. If you are nervous, still try to smile – firstly, it will calm you down, secondly, an exam that starts in a good atmosphere is usually better than a tense one.

For this reason, exams usually start with an easy question – your date of birth and your programme of study for the protocol.

In literature, oral exams often start with a short presentation on a text you have prepared. In your presentation, you should be able to

- provide a **context** for a given text (period, genre, historical background if helpful), and identify some typical **features**,
- characterize the **language** and **style** of a given text,
- note **parallels** to the texts you have read in class,
- use the **terminology** of literary theory with confidence,
- replace descriptive summaries by **abstract conclusions.** Do not summarize any plots if you are not specifically asked to do that. Instead, draw abstract conclusions from concrete observation in the text.

**Example:**

- **Concrete observation:** Mabel worries about her ugly yellow dress. She cannot talk to people at the party and leaves early.
- **Abstract conclusion:** Mabel worries about her dress because the other women at the party make her feel inadequate. Isolation of characters such as Mabel is typical of modernist writing.

Talk loudly and clearly. If you tend to talk relatively fast, remember to pause more frequently. This gives both you and your audience time to think, which is even more important in an oral exam than in an in-class presentation. If you talk too fast, not only may the examiner miss an important bit, but you will be asked many more questions than your fellow students, which increases chances the examiner will pick a question you cannot answer. Students tend to think they have to answer questions right away, which is not exactly true. You may take a moment to think before you answer complex questions. You may let the examiner know you have understood the question by saying something like: "What an interesting aspect. Let me consider this for a moment…"

The more you are able to differentiate between several aspects of the question, the more professional you come across. Questions such as "Is Modernism rather a beginning, an ending, or a period of transition?" seldom can be answered by picking one of the three. What you are expected to do is evaluate all three alternatives.

Be aware that in an oral exam, your lecturer may not phrase his or her questions as carefully as in a written exam. Sometimes, you are faced with questions as vague as "Could you tell us something about…?". When asked to "describe" a theory, such as Lacanian psychoanalysis, students tend to list facts and characteristics. This is the correct way of proceeding in a written

exam. In an oral exam, the expectation may be slightly different – the examiner might, if only on a subconscious level, think
you should also be aware of the criticism and shortcomings of
psychoanalysis. On the one hand, he or she may be disap-
pointed if you stop here. On the other hand, if you keep talking
about Kristeva for ten minutes now, the examiner might think
you are unable to answer a precise question. In such a case, it
is perfectly OK to add: "Lacanian psychoanalysis has been se-
verely criticized, especially by feminists. Would you like me to
go into more detail here?" If your examiner takes the hint,
congratulations, this is another question you can answer, and
time is on your side. If your examiners decline, it is alright because you have obviously told them what they wanted to hear.

You cannot manoeuvre your examiner through the whole
exam, but you can still drop some subtle hints, or ask them
to clarify questions you have not understood.

After the exam, you are asked to leave the room and wait
outside until the examiners have decided on a grade. Do not
worry if it takes a while – they might just be discussing whether your exam went very well or excellent. According to the
standards required by quality control at universities, grading
criteria should be made transparent during the course, definitely before the exam. There may be special requirements
related to the level of study and the type of course, however,
the following grading criteria are applied to most oral exams:

- **Accuracy.** Facts, data, details, and terminology are fully
  accurate. You are not making anything up.
- **Depth.** You do not state the obvious ("Macbeth is a bad
  person and must be punished"), but draw conclusions that
  help your analysis ("Macbeth's downfall is due to *hamar-
  tia*, his 'vaulting ambition', and his misinterpretation of the
  witches' predictions"). You know the key concepts and
  underlying theories, effortlessly relating them to social,
  cultural and historical situations. You avoid clichés.

- **Knowledge of texts.** You have read all texts required for the course and remember the names of the characters, the plots, the general themes.
- **Organisation.** Your arguments are logical, you do not jump between different topics. A person who did not attend the class would be able to follow your train of thought.
- **Language.** You use terminology correctly and confidently. Your English is accurate enough to bring across your meaning.

## Exercises

### Exercise 11.1
**Exam regulations.** What is your programme of study? Look up exam regulations for your final exam. Of how many parts does it consist? Which parts are written exams? How much time do you have?

### Exercise 11.2
**Jeopardy!** Find the correct exam instructions to the following answers, using the correct instructive verbs. You may need some of the following: assess, compare, contrast, define, describe, explain, illustrate, outline, state.

a) Both Romeo and Tybalt are young, temperamental, and easily offended.
b) Whereas Macbeth feels guilty after the murder of Duncan and seems paralyzed, all Lady Macbeth can think of is hiding the daggers.
c) The exposition is the first act of a drama, introducing the characters and their situation.
d) Mr Hyde is a pale, dwarfish man. He looks like a cave-dweller and speaks in a hissing voice. Hyde is violent and aggressive.

e) Although he is not a main character, Doctor Lanyon is extremely important for the plot. He raises the issue of ethics, and it is in his presence that the reader first witnesses the transformation of Hyde into Jekyll.

**Exercise 11.3**
**Multiple Choice.** Tick all correct answers that apply. Do not give up if you are not sure about the answer. For each question, decide on a suitable strategy.

11.3.1  What kinds of exam questions will get you the most points?

a)  General knowledge                                               ❑
b)  Solving a problem                                               ❑
c)  Reproductive knowledge                                         ❑
d)  Knowledge transfer                                             ❑

11.3.2  Which statement(s) about **plagiarism** is/are **true**?

a)  Submitting someone else's paper as yours
    is plagiarism.                                                 ❑
b)  Quoting a proverb without a source is plagiarism.             ❑
c)  Using a spelling checker is plagiarism.                       ❑
d)  Paraphrasing someone else's ideas is plagiarism.             ❑

11.3.3  Which of the following statements correspond(s) **to current MLA style** (8th edition)?

a)  The title of a **poem** is written in double
    quotation marks.                                              ❑
b)  The title of a **short story** is written in italics.        ❑
c)  The title of a **journal article** is written in double
    quotation marks.                                              ❑
d)  The title of an **anthology** is written in italics.         ❑

# Chapter 12: Out of sight, Out of Mind? The Art of Giving and Receiving Feedback

Finally, please imagine the following situation: it is Saturday evening. The weather is bad, and most of your friends are busy (probably still pouring over their research papers). You have just made yourself comfortable in front of the TV, stocked up with drinks and snacks for the evening. For lack of any better idea, you zap into a well-known casting show. The candidate rocks the stage with a performance that thrills the audience. Maybe he is not a real pop star yet, but his performance is still quite promising, you think. The song is over and the candidate leaves the stage. Wait a minute. Something is missing! He didn't listen to the judges' verdict at all! There are four judges who are successful within the very same industry that the likeable candidate wants to join. They are paid to watch his performance and give him a few tips for his future career. They followed his vocal coaching, his development since the rehearsals, and his performance attentively and took some notes. Nevertheless, he does not even ask their opinion. He is not the only one. In this strange casting show, nine out of ten candidates pass by the judges' desk unerringly.

Because this show seems strange to you, you switch to a much-loved quiz show. For the inconspicuous-looking candidate in the grey blouse, it's about one million euros. "Which of these people was born the same year as Queen Elizabeth II?" You too can hardly decide between A) Audrey Hepburn, B) Judy Garland, C) Julie Andrews, and D) Marilyn Monroe.[1] You saw

---

[1]   This was the one million pound question on *Who Wants to Be a Millionaire?* of 1st September 2019, asked to retired geography teacher Davyth Fear. Charlie Millward, "Who Wants to be Be a Millionaire Viewers Astrounded". Web. 28 September 2019. <https://www.express.co.uk/showbiz/tv-radio/1172665/Who-Wants-to-Be-a-Millionaire-Jeremy-Clarkson-contestant-winnings-half-

*The Wizard of Oz* and *Mary Poppins* when you were a child, and you know these films are relatively old; you have a dim memory of Marilyn Monroe in her white dress stepping onto a subway grate, maybe you have even walked over Audrey Hepburn's star on the Walk of Fame during your gap year in California. How old exactly was the Queen, again? To be honest, you have no idea. The young lady eventually settles for Marilyn Monroe.

You're holding your breath. Will a glittering rain fall from the studio ceiling, or will there be long faces? Neither. The young lady rises from her chair, thanks the host politely, and says: "I'm going home now. Whether I was right or not, I'll find out anyway when I get my bank statement".

Not likely to happen? Well, at least not on television. Although one cannot compare a seminar paper with a casting show on television, it is noticeable that, for most students, the seminar paper is over and done with as soon as the deadline has expired. The principle "out of sight, out of mind" seems to apply. Since the grades are recorded electronically, it is no longer absolutely necessary to go to the office hour in order be assessed.

It is incomprehensible that those who drop in to look at their papers are almost exclusively those whose work was graded as first class. Others rarely review their papers, although there are very few cases on file in which students were devoured by lecturers due to chronic susceptibility to error…

It remains a fact that in a seminar of 20 participants a lecturer writes down a detailed assessment of 20 assignments and considers for all 20 what advice he or she could give them for the next assignment; in the end this feedback is only communicated to one or two course participants because the rest of the course cannot be bothered to ask for feedback.

---

million-ITV-video>. You can find the answer to the million pound question in the Solutions section of this volume.

You have invested a lot of time and effort in your research paper. Your lecturers have invested just as much time and effort in adequately assessing and documenting your results and have thought intensely about how you could improve your performance. Both have wasted their time if the debriefing is just cancelled.

It does not matter how full your timetable for the semester is; be sure to take the opportunity for a debrief! There is no denying that the teachers are also under time pressure and that it can sometimes take a few days before you get a debriefing appointment, especially if it is outside the official office hours. It remains a fact, however, that supervision (and debriefing) is part of the job description. Your lecturers are there to explain mistakes and give you suggestions for improvement, a 'service' which has already been done with the correction and which you only have to pick up. Ask us: where have you succeeded in your academic work? What has not been quite as brilliant? What should you do differently for the next assignment?

No one will rip your head off if not every argument is one hundred per cent convincing and not every footnote is in the right place. Feedback and criticism are important for your own progress. Since you have to submit written work in many courses, you should draw conclusions from the debriefing about how to approach your next paper.

Unhappy with your grade? Unless the examiner or supervisor has made an obvious mistake – that does happen, we are all human – it is no use arguing. If your perception varies from your examiner's, what is important is that you know why. Be respectful even if you disagree, try not to slam the door. It is legitimate to ask what you could have done better, what was missing in your answer. Take notes and keep them with your important documents, as you will want to consult them before your next exam. In case the examiner does not provide any useful feedback, chalk it off as experience. You will do better next time.

Do not be annoyed by past mistakes, but develop strategies to avoid them in the future. If you have not seen the paper in the introductory course, you are likely to make the same mistakes in the advanced seminar. In a worst-case scenario, you will find yourself pouring over the Bachelor's thesis, still not knowing the difference between italics and quotation marks. Such gaps in knowledge are embarrassing for exam candidates and can have serious consequences for the assessment of your written work. Therefore, create a solid basis for academic writing during your first term papers.

If you have worked through the exercises and hints in this book, you have already taken the first step of this journey.

# Appendix

## Solutions

## Solutions Chapter 1

### Exercise 1.1
The best thing to do before filling in the matrix is look at your calendar of November and mark important dates (yes, this is called transfer – it was in the text of this chapter, but not in the part about the Eisenhower matrix).

| Mon | | 1 | 8 translation due, library tour | 15 |
|-----|-----------|--------|---------------------------------|-----------|
| Tue | | 2 | 9 literature presentation | 16 |
| Wed | | 3 | 10 test, word proc. class | 17 reading due |
| Thu | | 4 | 11 | 18 |
| Fri | 29 do dishes | 5 | 12 | 19 |
| Sat | 30 shop for Halloween | 6 yoga | 13 | 20 |
| Sun | 31 Halloweeen | 7 yoga | 14 | 21 |

Looking at the schedule, you will note several problems. Shopping for Halloween would not normally be considered urgent, but given that it is Friday and Halloween is on a Sunday when most shops are closed, it needs your immediate attention. What makes things worse is that the yoga class you want to attend takes up the whole weekend before your busiest week: you have a deadline for a translation, a presentation, and a language test. In addition to that, you may choose to go on a guided tour of the library. You may want to think about re-scheduling the less urgent tasks of the word processing class and the library tour to a less busier time.

There is not one correct solution to the problem because your priorities vary individually. Some people might argue they will cancel the yoga class to study, others might think the relaxation at the yoga class is just the thing they need before a busy week. This is a suggestion for structuring the schedule:

As you can see, the difficulty is that everything that will really help you achieve your long-term goal – success in your studies – has been categorized as "important, but not ur-gent". It is likely that you will get all the C-tasks done long before you even start doing research for your term paper. You have got two weeks to read *To the Lighthouse*, the relatively thin volume looks manageable in comparison to the six hun-dred pages of *Jane Eyre* you read last semester, so you will most likely class it as a B-task. The trouble is: you do not know how difficult to read it might be, or when exactly you are going to set aside time for reading. Most likely, you will not start reading until after your language test, which gives you a meagre six days for 170 pages of demanding Modernist writing. That is why many students will show up with a book they have not finished reading. Without some discipline and long-term planning, you will never accomplish all tasks with-in a sensible time frame. In fact, it is advisable to start reading your primary texts before the beginning of the semester (and take notes about what you have read).

C-tasks are things that have to be done soon – the dishes may start to smell, shops may close –, but that does not mean you have to do them alone. If you really are on a tight sched-ule, try to delegate these tasks. There are three of you at your student apartment, so why do you have to do the shopping and choose the music? Divide the tasks among yourselves. Make a schedule for household duties and stick to it (if you ask your housemate to do your dishes just this once, you have to return the favour at the next opportunity, of course!).

|  | urgent |  |
|---|---|---|
| important | A<br>translation<br>study for language test<br>presentation | B<br>term paper<br>word processing class<br>library tour<br>read *To the Lighthouse*<br>study for end-of-term<br>tests |
|  | C<br>do the dishes<br>shop for Halloween<br>dentist's appointment | D<br>newsletters and social<br>networks<br>redecorate kitchen<br>yoga workshop |

## Exercise 1.2

In this example, three tasks have been categorized as D, "not urgent, not important" (of course, that would depend on your stress level and the state of your kitchen). Time management guide books usually advise you to drop D tasks from your schedule altogether. Do you really need to read the newsletter about 30% discount on dog chow at the local supermarket? Do you even want to see your best friend from kindergarten post her lunch on a social network? If you have answered these two questions with a 'yes', at least think about reducing such activities, or scheduling them for a time when you are less efficient. Not all tasks of the D category, however, can be put off forever. At one point, your kitchen will need decorating, or you will definitely want some downtime. Consider paying someone to redecorate your kitchen, and schedule a regular time slot for yoga. Instead of investing a whole weekend, why not find an evening class once a week?

## Exercise 1.3

The dentist's appointment is a regular task that comes up twice a year, so try to make it a habit to always go to the dentist in the same two time slots, ideally when you do not have classes or exams to worry about. The library tour takes place on every first Monday of a month during term, so there is no need to schedule it in November if you are so busy. As your presentation is due the same week, the tour is not likely to be of much use at this point any more. Do not put it off infinitely – save a date for the library tour, maybe the second Monday of December. This is early enough to help you with research for your research paper. The word processing classes are offered on several concrete dates: Wed 10 November, Sat 15 January, Wed 9 February, Tue 1 March. As this is an appointment that takes a whole day, you should choose a date on which you will not miss a class. As you have a test on 10 November, this will not work. The other dates offered all fit into your schedule, however, it may not be advisable to sign up for 9 February, as your exams will take place during that week. March will be too late for your term paper, which is due only two weeks later. Therefore, the best choice may be 15 January.

## Solutions Chapter 2

## Exercise 2.1

a) A good topic. "Aspects" shows that individual focal points can be selected here. The framework, Jane Austen's best-known novel, is manageable. The scope of the paper, the Regency period, is limited.

b) The word "representations" already contains the idea that these are images/representations. The proposed theme is therefore tautological. Better: The Representation of Women in Shakespeare's *Othello* and Blake Morrison's *The Last Weekend*.

c) The subject matter is far too broad. Psychoanalysis is not just Freud, but also Jung and Lacan, to mention just a few. Your title should already specify what kind of psychoanalysis you are talking about. Furthermore, in your paper, you should point out the limits of such an approach and the extensive criticism of psychoanalytical approaches (Cixous, Kristeva).

d) The topic allows different approaches. Do you want to focus on witches, on Macbeth and his lady, on evil in a warlike, patriarchal society? Everything is possible here, from an analysis of the witch motif to a philosophical discussion of the theodicy question. It would be better to lower our sights: "Studies on the Role of Evil in *Macbeth*". With this you do not claim to want to cover everything.

e) This subject is much too narrow. At least you should look at blood imagery in the entire drama. Consider expanding the topic to "Metaphors of Violence in *Macbeth*".

f) The title is too long and confusing. An alternative proposal must mention the essential aspect of the analysis. It would be advisable to shorten the list of novels and find a catchy title, for example: "A Recipe for Terror – Fear in Radcliffe's *Mysteries of Udolpho* and Dacres *Zofloya*", or, in the case of more than two novels, "in Selected Gothic Novels".

g) A good subject in itself. It could, however, prove difficult to filter out the most important current publications in the jungle of secondary literature. For this reason, one should take advantage of the support offered at your university when considering such a topic.

h) Unsuitable: this is a subjective evaluation. It would be better to focus the analysis on the objections and accusations of later feminists to Wollstonecraft's approach: "Feminist Critique of Mary Wollstonecraft's *A Vindication of the Rights of Woman*".

## Exercise 2.2

Central terms in the topic: a GOOD term paper, WRITING
   Starting from these, you may begin your brainstorming session:

– Good: clarity, conciseness, discovering new aspect, originality, suitable sources, structure, interesting topic, convincing conclusion, …
– Writing: orthography, grammar, spelling checker, expression, academic register, no contractions, keep to formal requirements, MLA style, proper citation, word processing…

## Solutions Chapter 3

### Exercise 3.1

a) yes (review of a book in the online edition of a paper)
b) no (private website, many mistakes such as "copywright" imply that there is no peer-review or other form of quality control)
c) no (fansite, no academic background required, can be edited by anyone)
d) yes (project of the University of Singapore, authors are experts)
e) yes (museum homepage, compiled by scholars)
f) no (the author Amanda Mabillard is an academic and even provides guidance on how to quote in MLA style, however, her sources are not indicated in the correct places they are quoted at. The author's ideas are not clearly sep-

arated from her secondary sources. Pupils reading Shake-speare in school may look at those pages to improve their understanding of individual scenes, however, the analysis is too superficial to cover the aspects you would need to discuss in a research paper at university).

**Exercise 3.2**
a) For what purposes would you use the following sources in your academic work?
   - Online encyclopaedia (*e.g. Wikipedia*): study on online culture/Web 2.0/ 'editing wars' in Cultural Studies.
   - conference proceedings: current state of research
   - *ODNB:* biography of a British author, artist, politician, monarch
   - *MLA International Bibliography*: identify texts that were written about your topic
b) Where would you look?
   - Freud's model of the psyche was briefly mentioned in the seminar, but you do not know what it is: lexicon
   - You need a brief description of Freud's model of the psyche for a footnote in your paper: handbook article, overview of literary theory (such as Barry, Bertens, Klages)
   - You are writing a paper analysing Henry James' *The Turn of the Screw* from a psychological point of view and need a body of theory on Freudian psychoanalysis: spe-cialized books and articles on the topic; check the *MLA International Bibliography*, other databases, and your library catalogue.

**Exercise 3.3**
a) A zeugma is using a word in a sentence once, but in two separate contexts with separate meanings, for example: "Here thou, great Anna! whom three realms obey,/ Dost

sometimes Counsel take – and sometimes Tea" (Alexander Pope, *The Rape of the Lock*, Canto III).

A zeugma is a stylistic figure, so you can look it up in a glossary of literary terms, for example: Abrams, M.H. and Geoffrey Halt Harpham, *A Glossary of Literary Terms.* Boston: Cengage, 2015.

b) The most prominent representative of New Historicism is Stephen Greenblatt.

You could find what you are looking for in an introduction to literary theory, as long as it takes New Historicism into account, for example:

Barry, Peter. *Beginning Theory. An Introduction to Literary and Cultural Theory. Fourth Edition* Manchester: Manchester UP, 2017.

c) To find publications on a specific topic in professional journals, you should start a search query on the *MLA International Bibliography* database. Then, for example, you will come across Gunby, Ingrid. "*History in Rags: Adam Thorpe's Reworking of England's National Past*". Contemporary Literature 44.1 (Spring, 2003): 47-72.

d) Check the *MLA International Bibliography* for Catherine Spooner (author field) AND Dark Shadows. The publication is called "'Last Night I Dreamt I Went to Collinwood Again': Vampire Adaptation and Reincarnation Romance in *Dark Shadows*". *Horror Studies* 8.2 (2017): 205-222.

e) Gerard Manley Hopkins was a nineteenth-century poet. Use the *ODNB*.

f) Various answers are possible, depending on the classification of the literary history used. The *Norton Anthology of English Literature* classifies texts between 1789 (French Revolution) and 1818 (publication of Mary Shelley's *Frankenstein*) as Romantic, Seeber limits Romanticism by the years 1798 (appearance of the *Lyrical Ballads*) and 1820 (death of Scott), some poets frequently referred to as the

'Big Six' of Romanticism are Wordsworth, Coleridge, Blake, Shelley, Keats, and Byron.

g) This may sound a bit like Oscar Wilde, but it is, in fact, Lord Byron ("Byron and Shelley on the Character of Hamlet". *The New Monthly Magazine and Literary Journal* 29 (1830): 327-336, 328). Look up quotes in the *Oxford Dictionary of Quotations*.

## Solutions Chapter 4

### Exercise 4.1
**Situation 1:** Bring your own laptop, along with suitable cables and adapters. If that is impractical, save your file in several formats, including older programme versions (*e.g.* .ppt and .pptx) and PDF, which can be transferred to all platforms. You will lose fancy effects or animations, but you retain the content of your slides.

**Situation 2:** Your fellow students are either bored or preoccupied with something beyond your control, such an impeding exam. Try to draw their attention back to your presentation by doing something unexpected, such as involving them by activating methods.

**Situation 3:** As difficult as that may be: wait a moment until they turn off the jackhammer. Otherwise you will just have to repeat what you said. Look on the bright side: a pause will enhance the dramatic effect.

**Situation 4:** Aim for balance here. Neither expose those students who have not read the text, nor bore those who have with an elaborate summary. Instead, spontaneously drop a few subtle hints on the plot and characters ("Jane, who is the protagonist Lizzy's sister, as you will probably remember…)

## Exercise 4.2

a) "Could you define what you understand by a 'good' text?" (There is a whole discipline concerned with the 'value' of literary texts, which is called axiology).

b) "Which part of my arguments precisely did you not find conclusive?"

c) "Gladly, however, I am not sure everybody in this room remembers E.M. Forster in detail. Maybe you could briefly highlight the aspects of Forster's writing you would like me to compare XY with?" If you feel, however, that this strategy of distraction might not work, maybe because it was your lecturer who asked the question, grab a pen and say: "Thank you for this question. I was going to look into it for my research paper. Let me take a short note."

## Solutions Chapter 5

**In his gripping 2010 novel *The Last Weekend***: "gripping" is a personal assessment that has no place in academic writing.

**Ian, a married primary school teacher who's invited by his snobbish university friend Ollie for a country weekend**: This is a re-telling of the plot. As you can assume your readers know the text, you can dispense with such explanations in a brief abstract. In addition, the contraction "who's" is not used in formal, written English.

**Ian strives to establish a bond with the reader. Yet a thinly-disguised agenda of self-justification questions Ian's reliability even before intertextual evidence links him to Iago**: If you include the concept of intertextuality, you should at least briefly explain what theoretical basis you want to work with, such as Bakhtin or Kristeva.

**Thus the reader asks himself: why does Ian betray both his friend Ollie and the reader, and how is the motif of betrayal linked to Shakespeare's drama?**: It is not entirely unproblematic to use the term "the reader" here without further reflection or commentary. What 'reader' are you talking about? Is this a subjective question that you have personally asked yourself? Are you talking about the 'implied reader' by Wolfgang Iser? You should also avoid asking direct questions in your abstract.

**Echoes of Shakespeare's *Othello* pervade Morrison's novel: the names of the protagonists, Ian, Ollie, Daisy, Emily.** It is not necessary to give all examples in the abstract. Reduce information to the essentials.

**In this paper, I am going to show that *The Last Weekend* is not a simple re-working of *Othello*:** The "I" should not appear in academic texts. Omit the first part of the sentence: "*The Last Weekend* is not a simple re-working of *Othello*".

**which makes people prone to betrayal when their ambitions are at stake:** "make" is colloquial. Better: "people tend to betray each other".

## Solutions Chapter 6

### Exercise 6.1
There is no right or wrong answer to a reading response, but the following structure is suggested by the question:

- Brief summary of the poem (speaker, friend, situation)
- Description of two types of knowledge
- Assessment
- (possibly: personal conclusions)

### Example:
The speaker of the poem, William, is reproached by his good friend Matthew because William spends the day outside instead of studying. Matthew believes that William is wasting

his time, but William insists that nature can teach him a different kind of knowledge which cannot be learnt from books. There are two quite different types of knowledge mentioned in the poem:

Matthew is a strong believer in accumulative knowledge, which means gathering facts from books, "that light bequeathed/ To Beings else forlorn and blind" (l. 5) – without books, there can be no education because the only way to increase one's knowledge is learning from one's elders and betters: " the spirit breathed/ From dead men to their kind" (l. 7-8).

William is drawn towards nature to gain intuitive knowledge, which is within every individual and can only be discovered if one's senses are stimulated by nature. As human beings cannot stop seeing, hearing, or feeling (ll. 17.-20), it is not necessary to actively seek knowledge; all that is required is an open mind and the impressions of nature: " we can feed this mind of ours/ In a wise passiveness" (ll. 23-24).

It is quite obvious that, to the speaker of the poem, the intuitive kind of knowledge inspired by nature is more important. Matthew characterizes the advice of ancient authors to their students as "spirit breathed/ From dead men to their kind" (ll. 7-8), which is paradoxical because dead people are unable to breathe. Furthermore, the verse implies that students of the ancients, such as Matthew, are dead already without realizing it because they are wasting their lives over books. It is William who possesses knowledge which is truly valuable, being in tune with nature.

It is, however, doubtful whether the assessment is correct today; hard facts are required for all professions, and those can only be learned from books and experts in the field. One would not want the surgeon to remove an appendix based on intuition inspired by a walk in the park.

## Exercise 6.2

Where as a reading response is usually based on the primary text only, more context and additional sources would be required. You would need books on the Romantic Age and the role of nature, as well as the role-model of the ancients and its importance for Neoclassicists (Matthew seems to share their views, whereas William is a Romantic). Back up your own ideas with what you can find in books and articles. For a term paper, you might want to compare the poem to other works by Wordsworth, such as "The Tables Turned". Furthermore, an essay or term paper would be more objective, whereas much of a reading response is your impression of the text. The final paragraph would have to be rewritten, moving away from your personal view to a scholarly assessment: how did the Victorians question the Romantic views of intuitive knowledge, what changed in English society?

## Solutions Chapter 7

## Exercise 7.1
a) The War of the Worlds (preposition 'of' and article 'the' are spelt with small letters)
b) The Old Man and the Sea ('and' is a coordinating conjunction)
c) The House on Mango Street (preposition 'on' is spelt with a small letter)
d) Staying On (to 'stay on' is a phrasal verb, meaning 'staying longer, continue in a place')
e) Men without Women ('without' is a preposition here, not an adverb; *cf.* "What are the five things you can't live without?")
f) Nineteen Eighty-Four ('four', the second part of the numeral, is also capitalized). Some authors will capitalize prepositions consisting of more than four letters.

## Exercise 7.2

### a) From the introduction: John Fowles, *The French Lieutenant's Woman*

The introduction begins with a central aspect, but it contains too many sweeping judgments. There are neither "the Victorians" nor "the women", "the Christians", nor "the Europeans". Society as a whole cannot be religious, but religion can exert a strong social influence, which one must prove if one makes such an assertion. Although it is true that sexuality has been discussed less frequently in the public sphere than in today's England, nevertheless the density of brothels in the big cities, for example, remains unconsidered in this approach. The generalization that marriage and family are no longer a priority of 'the modern woman' is unacceptable. The assertion that gender discrimination no longer exists is certainly correct in relation to human rights established in many democratic constitutions, but it ignores factors such as the "glass ceiling" in senior management, or cultures not subscribing to the equality of the sexes. Differentiate instead of judging from superficial impressions.

### b) From the Main Part: Role of Intertextuality in John Fowles, *The Collector*

This section seems very insecure. The author obviously does not want to commit himself, since he constantly uses phrases like "seems", "may well" or "it remains unclear whether". If your assertion is wrong, however, it will not help that you were not sure. If your assertion is correct, you are depriving it of all persuasiveness. Take a clear position and substantiate your statements with primary and secondary literature. While it is possible to prove through secondary literature that an imagination such as Frederick's, in which a kidnapping victim begins to identify with the perpetrator, can occur psychologically (Stockholm Syndrome), the text excludes this assumption in Miranda's case. Prove this with appropriate statements from the text in which Miranda gives free rein to her despair and hatred of the perpetrator.

c) **From the Concluding Part: Role of Intertextuality in John Fowles, *The Collector***

This conclusion does not sum up anything. It begins with a subjective evaluation – original, constantly surprising. This is not very academic – if you want to say something about the unexpected in the novel, be more precise, for example referring to plot twists, a changing narrative perspective, postmodern ludism, intertextuality.

If your topic is intertextuality in *The Collector*, it is not enough to write that there allusions to other texts in the novel. You have (hopefully) elaborated on the forms and functions of intertextuality in detail in your analytical part and should now draw a conclusion. Have you identified appropriate passages in the text, what are the effects? The last sentence is the attempt at an outlook, but unfortunately this outlook does not consist of ideas for further topics of investigation, but continues the plot; who will be murdered now? This is not what you are supposed to accomplish.

d) **From the Concluding Part: Concepts of Masculinity in *Othello***

The author again tries to give an outlook. This fails because he apologizes for having analysed only two characters, according to the motto "it would go beyond the scope of this paper". You had a reason for narrowing down the scope of your theme; you concluded that Iago and Othello were suitable for demonstrating concepts of masculinity, otherwise you would have chosen other characters. Stand up for your work with confidence, but point beyond it. Why would a subsequent analysis of Brabantio, Roderigo and Cassio be profitable for research? Who has already written such an analysis?

## Solutions Chapter 8

### Exercise 8.1

a) True.
b) False (no quotation marks).
c) False.
d) False, corrections must be marked.
e) False, it is better to start with a quote and end with a great idea of your own.
f) False, only if the original source is unavailable.
g) True.
h) False, you have to place the letter you changed in square brackets.

### Exercise 8.2

Thomas Spence, born in Newcastle upon Tyne in 1750, was the son of Scottish parents and one of nineteen children (Mackenzie 399-400). His father, a netmaker, being a deeply religious man, insists on his sons learning to read from the Bible (*ibid.*).

> *ibid.* means that information about Spence's father can also be found in the aforementioned source.

Spence's convictions were influenced by the Glassite sect, *i.e.* a Protestant group known for its advocacy of communal ownership of property.

Unlike other eighteenth-century philosophers with an upper-class upbringing, *e.g.* William Godwin, Spence addressed his texts to an audience comprised of peasants and craftsmen.

> *i.e.* means 'that is', whereas *e.g.* means 'for example'.

Human rights are established in Spence's 1803 *Constitution of Spensonia*: "Government is instituted to secure to man the enjoyment of his natural and impresceptable [*sic!*] rights" (166).

> Probably this should be 'imprescriptible', but as it is spelt differently in your source material, add [*sic*!] so people will not think this is your mistake.

The economic independence of women from their husbands and fathers is one of the greatest advancements of Spence's political utopias. Some authors, however, argue that they still reflect the type of conservative, passive female behaviour characteristic of eighteenth-century English society (*cf.* Duthille 21).

> *Cf.* refers to a source representing a different view.

## Solutions Chapter 9

### Exercise 9.1

a) The murder of Duncan, which was the idea of Macbeth's wife, is a serious crime. Commas should be used instead of dashes because dashes are used to indicate a break in the sentence, whereas this is just a non-defining relative clause.

b) Macbeth believes he will not have to justify himself; he is, however, wrong.
   In this sentence, the author clearly refers to the character, not the play. Macbeth therefore should not be in italics. Furthermore, the short form "won't" should be replaced by "will not". Finally, the second sentence should not start with "But".

c) In my first e-mail, I had forgotten the attachment, but I re-sent it. The hyphen in "re-sent" is important here because its omission changes the meaning of the sentence: "re-send" = send again, "resent" = dislike.

d) You think you know everything about punctuation – but is that really true? In this example, there should be a dash instead of a hyphen.

## Exercise 9.2

The following solution is just a suggestion, not taking account of optional elements (such as the performers of *Robin of Sherwood*, the original date of Barack Obama's speech) or varying editions.

### MLA7:

Daston, Lorraine. "Curiosity in Early Modern Science". *Word and Image* 11/4 (1995): 391-404. Print.

Hutcheon, Linda. *A Poetics of Postmodernism: History, Theory, Fiction.* New York and London: Routledge, 1998. Print.

Obama, Barack. "Full Transcript: President Barack Obama's Inaugural Address". *ABC News*. Web. 17 August 2019. <http://abcnews.go.com/Politics/Inauguration/president-obama-inauguration-speech-transcript/story?id=6689022>.

Rumbold, Valerie. "Pope and Gender". *The Cambridge Companion to Alexander Pope*. Ed. Pat Rogers. Cambridge: CUP, 2007. 199-209. Print.

"The Swords of Wayland Part 2". *Robin of Sherwood – The Complete Series. Director's Cut.* Writ. Richard Carpenter. Dir. Robert Young. Network, 2010. DVD.

### MLA8:

Daston, Lorraine. "Curiosity in Early Modern Science". *Word and Image,* vol. 11, no. 4, 1995, pp. 391-404.

Hutcheon, Linda. *A Poetics of Postmodernism: History, Theory, Fiction.* Routledge, 1998.

Obama, Barack. "Full Transcript: President Barack Obama's Inaugural Address". *ABC News*. 17 August 2019, http://abcnews.go.com/Politics/Inauguration/president-obama-inauguration-speech-transcript/story?id=6689022.

Rumbold, Valerie. "Pope and Gender". *The Cambridge Companion to Alexander Pope*, edited by Pat Rogers, CUP, 2007, pp. 199-209.

"The Swords of Wayland Part 2". *Robin of Sherwood – The Complete Series. Director's Cut*, written by Richard Carpenter, directed by Robert Young, Network, 2010.

## Solutions Chapter 10

### Exercise 10

a) Yes – someone else's ideas are passed off as one's own.
b) No, proofreading is allowed as well as the use of a dictionary or an automatic spelling checker.
c) No, it is a an acceptable tool, as is a dictionary of synonyms.
d) No, basic knowledge of your programme of study can be assumed to be familiar to your audience.
e) Yes, it is a collaborative effort of the course, not the interpretation of a person. If this is hijacked, the author claims the performance entirely for himself.
f) Yes – it is not enough to mention a source at the end of the chapter. If the entire chapter or a longer part of it is borrowed from another work, this must be clear. Otherwise: Only the last sentence of the chapter, the sentence with the source, is marked as someone else's intellectual property!
g) Yes – it is not enough to list the source in the bibliography, you must also indicate where you cited or paraphrased it in your work.
h) Yes – just the fact that it is not an academic source does not mean you can plagiarize it.

## Solutions Chapter 11

### Exercise 11.1
Individually

### Exercise 11.2
The correct instructions are:

a) Compare Romeo with Tybalt.
b) Contrast Macbeth and Lady Macbeth's behaviour after killing Duncan.
c) Define 'exposition'.
d) Describe Mr Hyde.
e) Assess the importance of Doctor Lanyon for the plot of *Strange Case of Dr Jekyll and Mr Hyde*.

### Exercise 11.3
11.3.1 What kinds of exam questions will get you the most points?
       b
       Strategy: Cover the answers with your hand. What would your answer be?

11.3.2 Which statement(s) about **plagiarism** is/are **true**?
       a and d
       Strategy: Eliminate nonsense answers. How would you ever find a source for a proverb? Would your lecturers really demand that you turn off the spelling checker, and how would they ever find out if you did? There is a fair chance that the remaining answers are correct.

11.3.3 Which of the following statements correspond(s) **to current MLA style** (8th edition)?
       a, c, and d

Strategy: Think of the rule: larger works: italics, smaller works published within a larger work: double quotation marks. Go through each of the answers one by one.

## Solutions Chapter 12

The correct answer is **D: Marilyn Monroe**. Both Marilyn Monroe and Queen Elizabeth II were born in 1926. The candidate Davyth Fear chose not to run the risk and won 500,000 pounds.

## Glossary

### Abstract                                      71, 86

1. Short summary of a given text. By writing abstracts of
   scholarly publications you read for your paper, you create
   a quick reference outlining the salient aspects of the book
   or article, which will accommodate your writing process.
   A plan of the project you are planning which highlights
   your understanding of the topic as well as the approaches
   and methods you intend to use in your research paper.
   Some instructors require you to write an abstract before
   you start writing. An abstract is a valuable tool to help you
   find the 'golden thread' which will run through your arguments.

### Anthology                                    147, 159
A collection of literary works which are too short to be published independently, by one or more authors, such as poetry
or short stories. It is generally preferable to quote these works
from their respective anthologies, rather than referring to
reprints in the press or on the internet.

### Axiology                                          218
A discipline within literary studies, concerned with the 'value'
of literature.

### Bibliography                        35, 49, 107, 147
List (in book form or as a database) of critical works available
on a particular author or subject. Consulting a Bibliography,
such as the *MLA International Bibliography*, is usually the first
step in a search for scholarly materials. Unlike a ➔ **library
catalogue**, however, a bibliography does not provide any
information on availability.

**Biographical Fallacy**                                    129, 190
Term coined by W.K. Wimsatt and M.C. Beardsley in 1976 to
denote the false impression that the meaning of a text can be
successfully decoded by accumulating biographical data
about its author.
   *Cf.* → **Intentional Fallacy**

**Biography**                                              24, 38, 46
A biography provides information about the life of an author
or another person of public interest, such as monarchs, politicians, artists, scientists, or philosophers. The *ODNB (Oxford
Dictionary of National Biography)* is one of the most frequently used biographical dictionaries in English.

**Block quote**                                            141, 158, 164
A quotation longer than three lines (MLA7) or three lines of
verse/ four lines of prose (MLA8) in a research paper, to be
formatted single-spaced and indented (0.5 inch or 1 cm).

**Chicago Style**                                          50
A style guide for American English regarding editorial practice,
such as formatting citations, notes, and bibliographical records. Chicago style offers two options of documentation:
notes-bibliography, and author-date.

**Citability (academically substantiated)**               139, 159
In order to be citable in an academic context, a published text
must follow the criteria of good academic practice and be
subjected to some form of quality control, *e.g.* peer-review,
or professional editing. For citations from literary texts, a
critical edition (if available) should be consulted.

### Citation; Quote                                    159
A literal reference to a source. In contrast to a paraphrase, a citation is formatted in quotation marks or indented as a block quote (frequently in a slightly smaller font).

### Clustering                                         27
Clustering is a structured method of brainstorming developed by Gabriele C. Rico for creative writing. Starting from a central topic, the writer groups his or her associations around the buzz word.

### Colloquial Language                        73, 85, 133
The common language spoken in everyday situations. Features of colloquial language include – but are not limited to – the use of contractions (*don't, can't*) and slang (*pal, gal, stuff*). Beginning a sentence with *And/But* is also part of colloquial language. It should be avoided in research papers.

### Colloquium
A group of researchers meet on a regular basis to discuss individual works in progress.

### Conference Proceedings                          33, 80
A collection of academic papers published subsequently to a scholarly conference on a particular topic. Contributors are speakers who presented their research at the conference. The proceedings reflect trends and currents within the scientific community and document the state of the art in their field.

### Copyright                                   40, 49, 175
The right to reproduce and publish one's works. Authors may sell copyright to a publisher, however, they retain → **Intellectual Property**. Copyright regulations vary by country. In the European Union, the copyright for a text expires 70 years after the death of its author, *i.e.* the text may be spread in the

public domain. The author's intellectual property, however, remains untouched – no one else may claim the text as their own (**→ Plagiarism**).

**Exception:** If the work was published posthumously, the editor retains copyright for the duration of 25 years.

**Course**                                                    15, 182
"Course" is an umbrella term for any class attended at university. Courses are differentiated into propaedeutic courses/introductory courses, lectures, seminars, and exam preparation courses.

**Deadline**                                      16, 20, 102, 206
Latest possible date of submission for an academic paper. Deadlines differ from university to university, in case of a term-paper encompassing a time span between 3 and 8 weeks from the end of a semester. Late submissions may be authorized by university administrations (*e.g.* in case of illness).

**Discursive Writing**                                          120
A style of writing which avoids one-dimensional or biased approaches to a given topic, but provides different, often diverging perspectives. Dialectic compositions employ a discursive writing technique, however, in academic papers, there cannot always be a synthesis representing a compromise. By writing in a discursive way, scholars demonstrate awareness of current debates and controversies in the scientific community and their own confident handling of the topic question.

**Dissertation, PhD Thesis**                              45, 51, 79
An academic paper which concludes a postgraduate programme leading to the academic degree of PhD (Germany: Dr. phil.). The demands of a dissertation exceed the level of a thesis concluding undergraduate programs and require a con-

siderably higher amount of skills in independent research and academic writing.

In Germany, the doctoral degree is not recognized and may not be used as a form of address until the doctoral certificate is in the possession of the candidate.

**Doctorate** 45

Postgraduate programme of study following the M.A. or teacher training in order to obtain the academic degree of PhD (Germany: Dr. phil.). Doctoral candidates are required to write an academic thesis of about 250 pages on a problem of their choice under the supervision of a professor (Germany: a *Privatdozent* may supervise doctoral candidates as long as the second supervisor is a professor). When the doctoral thesis has been accepted, the candidate defends it in an academic discussion commonly known as a "defence" (ca. 90 minutes). Doctorates can be obtained within a specific graduate school programme, a research training group, or independently with no formal association with a programme of study. A doctoral thesis must be published within a 2-year (exceptions: 4-year) time frame after the defence.

**Document Delivery** 37, 83

A service whereby you can order photocopies or scans of books or articles which are not available at your own library for a fee.

**Editor** 80, 160

The editor selects and organizes material for publication. The editor can, but need not be identical with the author.

**Essay** 41, 88, 159, 184

A form of academic writing with a structure less fixed and formal than a ➔ **Research Paper**. Derived from Latin *exa-*

*gium*, the essay denotes an 'attempt' to examine the depths of a question or problem

**Exposé**
Longer than an abstract, but shorter than the actual manuscript, an exposé provides the details and strategies of a research project. Exposés are usually written when looking for an academic advisor, applying for a PhD scholarship, or offering a manuscript to a publisher.

**Gender-Fair Language**                                                123
A type of politically correct language whose aim it is to eliminate gender bias from texts and speech.

**General Knowledge**                                                   172
General knowledge is held to be self-evident and need not be academically substantiated by → **Citation** or → **Paraphrase**.

**Grant, Loan**                                                      15, 19
As a student, you may apply for a grant or loan to pay for tuition fees and living costs.
    Grants, bursaries, and scholarships, which can come from the government, the university or private, political, and other non-profit organisations, do not have to be repaid. Loans have to be repaid, whereas terms and conditions vary. In Britain, students start repaying their Tuition Fee Loans and Maintenance Loans once their income exceeds a certain amount. In Germany, state grant (Bafög) recipients are obliged to start repaying five years after graduation, but up to 50% of the loan may become a grant for high achievers.
    The annual renewal of the grant or loan requires evidence of progress in the chosen programme of study.

**Handout**                                    56, 67, 174
A method to visualize information for the audience during a
seminar presentation, or to compile data and source material
for your fellow students to take home after your talk. Handouts should be clear and concise.

**Intellectual Property**                          169, 175
An author's or scholar's exclusive right to his own ideas.
Whereas authors can sell the right to reproduce and publish
their works **(→ Copyright),** they retain intellectual property.

**Intentional fallacy**                               135
A term coined by W.K. Wimsatt and M.C. Beardsley to denote
the false assumption that the meaning of a text is identical
with the author's intention, as in the phrase "What is the
author trying to tell us?". Current approaches in literary criticism recognize the impossibility of reconstructing the thought
processes of another person and call the author's authority
over the text into question. See also **→ Biographical fallacy**.
    See Wimsatt, W.K. and M.C. Beardsley, *On Literary Intention*.
Ed. David Newton-DeMolina, Edinburgh: Edinburgh UP, 1976.

**Interlibrary Loan, also: Interlibrary**
**Services (ILS)**                                 34, 45, 83
Option to loan books from a library which is not local, thus
expanding on the literature available at one's home university. Interlibrary loan is available either free of charge or for a
small fee, however, it requires early planning, as the ordering
process may take several weeks. If you require only a short
chapter or article, you can also order photocopies or scans
with a **→ document delivery** service.

**Introduction**                                      107
Short chapter at the beginning of an academic paper, which
outlines the topic for readers and limits the scope of the study

at hand. Introductions provide information about the texts, approaches, and methods used and consist of a descriptive text independent from the structure of the table of contents. Introductions should not simply be called "introduction", but have a formal headline.

**LaTex**                                                    156
A document preparation system. In contrast to WYSIWYG word processing systems, design and layout are separated from the content of a document. LaTex is frequently used for mathematical and technical research papers, but can be applied to any type of publication. *Cf*. <http://latex-project.org>.

**Library Catalogue**                                  34, 157
List of all works available at a local library or within a library association. Electronic catalogues frequently allow users to order books from affiliated libraries via ➔ **Interlibrary loan**. Unlike a bibliography, a library catalogue does not provide any information about publications not currently available to its patrons.

**List of Works Cited**                     67, 157, 162, 167
A comprehensive list of all sources quoted in an academic paper. Whereas the ➔ **Bibliography** lists all works and sources *consulted* during the writing process, the list of works cited implies that each source has been *quoted* at least once in the paper.

**Literary Studies, Literary Criticism**          84, 133
In English, the terms "Literary Studies" and "Literary Criticism" both denote the professional academic study and analysis of literature. It includes, but is not limited to literary theory and literary history.

The term 'literary criticism' is not to be confused with the German 'Literaturkritik', which only refers to the review of published books and does not involve any scholarly activity.

**Loan → Grant**

**Meta-Text**                                                          114, 130
Parts of a text in which an author comments on the writing process or the structure of the text.

Examples: "The theoretical chapter of this research paper is going to look at…", "Such a discussion would go beyond the scope of this paper". In academic writing, meta-text should be avoided.

**MLA Style**                                                      42, 50, 154, 157
A style guide issued by the *Modern Language Association* regarding editorial practice, such as formatting citations, notes and bibliographies.

**n.p., n.d., n.pag.**                                                      44
Abbreviations for 'no place', 'no date', 'not paginated' (= no page numbers). These are used when bibliographical data is missing, as is the case occasionally with older works (*n.p., n.d.*), websites which do not normally have page numbers, quotes from the dust jacket, or parts of a book that are not paginated.

**Patron**                                                          66, 237
A person who uses the services of a library. In Shakespeare's day, a patron was a person who financially supported a poet.

**Paraphrase**                                                          139, 171
Rephrasing of someone else's thought in your own words. Some styles (not including MLA style) mark all paraphrases consequently using *cf.*, as to distinguish them from direct citations.

Unlike quotations, paraphrases are not in quotation marks, but both require an academic source indicated in brackets, foot- or endnotes.

**Plagiarism**                                                    57, 134, 169
According to Waltman (whose definition is debatable): passing off someone else's thought or work as one's own or permitting them to be taken as such. Committing plagiarism will lead to the work being rejected. Further consequences such as removal from university, criminal persecution for fraud, or loss of academic titles may also apply. Plagiarism may be penalised in both cases of intentional (voluntary deception) and unintentional plagiarism (*e.g.* careless note-taking, loss of bibliographical information).

**Predatory Press**                                                          81
Colloquial term for publishers or journals ready to publish virtually any paper as long as the author is willing to pay their (usually very high) fees, without any form of quality control.

**(Course) Presentation, Speech**                              24, 34, 55
An oral presentation held by one or more students on a specific topic. The presentation may be graded. It is followed by a short Q & A section.

**Primary Literature**                                          38, 45, 74, 130
All texts used directly for literary analysis in a research paper.

**Publication (smaller works)**                                           159
A literary or academic piece of work published within another, larger piece of work, such as an article in a collection, or a poem in an anthology. In MLA Style, the titles of smaller publications are written in quotation marks.

### Publication (larger works) 159
A literary or academic piece of work published independently, *i.e.* not within another, larger piece of work. Examples for 'larger works' are novels, anthologies, and collections. In MLA style, the titles of larger works are written in italics.

### Research Training Group 43, 234
A peer-group in which young researchers, usually doctoral candidates and postdocs who work on loosely related projects, meet on a regular basis for information exchange and feedback. Research training groups offer a variety of workshops, conferences and seminars. Membership can be associated with a scholarship.

### Review 33, 42, 49, 82
The use of the word 'review' in literary and cultural studies differs from that of other disciplines.

A review in literary studies is an evaluation of a piece of work (literary or academic) employing a range of criteria (for a novel: entertainment factor, language and style, for an academic publication: academic accuracy and relevance within the scientific community).

N.B.: A review in medicine is a systematic overview, *e.g.* about a particular therapy.

### Scholarly Journal 36, 43, 48, 80
Highly specialized academic publication, quarterly or less frequent, in which scholars publish the most current findings in their fields of expertise. Journals are especially useful for research papers, as they best reflect the "state of the art".

### Scribal Abbreviations, Sigla 146, 164
Originally denoting symbols used by ancient scribes, scribal abbreviations in academic writing are symbols (often capital

letters) used to abbreviate primary sources in a scholarly text, such as *PP* for *Pride and Prejudice.*

**Secondary Literature**                     33, 38, 48, 65, 117
All sources used to substantiate the line of argument in an academic paper which are not part of the primary text itself. Secondary sources comprise scholarly publications and explanatory notes, but also philosophical, historiographical, or political texts which provide a context for the work at hand, other works of the same author, or similar works by different authors.

**Seminar**                                         46, 56, 97, 174
A course type with special emphasis on student research work. Unlike lectures, which focus on communicating knowledge to the students with relatively little interaction between the lecturer and the class, seminars provide guidance for students to develop their research skills. Seminars usually conclude with a paper of 10-12 pages in beginners', 15-20 pages in advanced students' seminars.

**Style sheets**                                    116, 153, 165
A style sheet (issued by the faculty or, later, a publisher) provides guidelines on formatting your paper in accordance with a specific style. Failure to abide by these guidelines may lead to a paper being rejected for formal reasons.

**Subjectivity**                                      24, 123, 132

1. Expressing one's own personal feelings or opinions is to be avoided in scholarly contents. Writers of research papers form an academic view based on the evidence and evaluation of their materials.
2. In literary studies the term 'subjectivity' refers to the degree of presence of the speaker in a poetic text (explicit *vs.* implicit subjectivity).

**Teacher Training**                                        96, 154

In some parts of Germany, students training to become teachers have a programme of study especially designed for them, concluding with the central exam of state of their respective *Bundesland*. These programmes overlap with the BA/MA programmes of the subjects studied, but are not identical.

Teacher training should not be confused with the separate subject of 'pedagogy', although schoolteachers are often colloquially referred to as 'pedagogues'.

**Term Paper/Research Paper**                          19, 26, 165

Paper of about 10 (beginning students) to 20 (advanced students) pages, in which students solve a topic question with the help of scholarly methods and sources, as well as present their findings in an academic style and register. Research papers are a common form of assessment in seminars at university.

**Thesis**                                          34, 41, 45, 51, 95

A longer research paper required to conclude a program of study and/or gain permission to take exams. The length of a thesis depends on the academic degree to be obtained (*e.g.* about 40 pages for a BA, 80-100 pages for an MA). Teacher training programmes in Germany usually require an admission thesis **(Zulassungsarbeit)**.

**Vanity Press, Vanity Publisher, Subsidy Publisher**      79

Other than trade publishers, vanity publishers demand that authors pay a printing cost subsidy to have their books published.

## Reference Works

Note: This list provides some orientation for students of English and American Studies. It is by no means exhaustive. Reading lists for your individual programme of study may be available from your department.

### Literary History (Ch. 3.8.1)

Baym, Nina, *e.a.* (ed.). *The Norton Anthology of American Literature.* London and New York: Norton, [8]2011.

Barnard, Robert. *A Short History of English Literature*. Hoboken, NJ: Wiley-Blackwell, [2]1994.

Greenblatt, Stephen *et al*. (eds.). The *Norton Anthology of English Literature.* London and New York: Norton, [9]2012.[1]

Sanders, Andrew. *The Short Oxford History of English Literature.* Oxford: OUP, 2002.

Widdowson, Peter. *The Palgrave Guide to English Literature and its Contexts*. Houndmills: Palgrave-Macmillan, 2004.

### Encyclopaedias of Authors, Biographies, Quotations (Ch. 3.8.2)

Abrams, M.H. and Stephen Greenblatt (eds.). *The Norton Anthology of English Literature. The Major Authors.* New York: Norton, 2001.

Drabble, Margaret. *The Oxford Companion to English Literature*. Oxford: OUP, 1985.

Knowles, Elizabeth. *Oxford Dictionary of Quotations*. Oxford: OUP, [8]2014.

---

[1]    Online: Eds. Eileen Connell (English Electronic Media Editor), Dale Hudson, Maeve Adams (review materials). 17 Apr 2019. <https://wwnorton.com/college/english/nael/welcome.htm>.

Matthew, H.C.G. (ed.). *Oxford Dictionary of National Biography*. Oxford: OUP, 2004.[2]

Scott-Kilvert, Ian. *British Writers*. New York: Scribner, 1992.

Shattock, Joanne. *The Oxford Guide to British Women Writers*. Oxford: OUP, 1993.

## Glossaries, Terminology, Handbooks (Ch. 3.8.3)

Abrams, M.H. and Geoffrey Galt Harpham. *A Glossary of Literary Terms*. Stamford, CT: Cengage, [11]2015.

Audi, Robert. *Cambridge Dictionary of Philosophy*. Cambridge: CUP, 2015.

Baldick, Chris (ed.). *The Oxford Dictionary of Literary Terms*. Oxford: OUP, [3]2008.

Blackburn, Simon. *The Oxford Dictionary of Philosophy*. Oxford: OUP, 2008.

Ferber, Michael. *A Dictionary of Literary Symbols*. Cambridge: CUP, 1999.

Groden, Michael, Martin Kreiswirth, and Imre Szeman (eds.). *The Johns Hopkins Guide to Literary Theory and Criticism*. Baltimore: Johns Hopkins UP, 1994.

Lanham, Richard. *A Handlist of Rhetorical Terms*. Berkeley, CA: University of California Press, [2]1991.

Lentricchia, Frank, and Thomas McLaughlin (eds.). *Critical Terms for Literary Study*. Chicago: University of Chicago Press, [2]1995.

Puchner, Martin. "Literary Terms". *The Norton Anthology of World Literature Online*. Web. 27 Apr 2019. <http://www.wwnorton.com/college/english/nawol3/literaryterms.aspx>.

---

[2]   Online: Oxford Dictionary of National Biography. OUP, 2019. <http://www.oxforddnb.com/>.

## Literary Theory (Ch. 3.8.4)

Bal, Mieke. *Narratology: Introduction to the Theory of Narrative.* Toronto: University of Toronto Press, ²1997.

Barry, Peter. *Beginning Theory. An Introduction to Literary and Cultural Theory.* Manchester: Manchester UP, ³2009.

Bertens, Hans. *Literary Theory. The Basics.* London: Routledge, ³2017.

Brooker, Peter, and Peter Widdowson. *A Practical Reader in Contemporary Literary Theory*. London: Longman, 1996.

Culler, John. *Literary Theory. A Very Short Introduction*. Oxford: Oxford UP, 2000.

Eagleton, Terry. *Literary Theory. An Introduction*. Minneapolis: University of Minnesota Press, 1996.

Guerin, Wilfred L. *e.a. A Handbook of Critical Approaches to Literature.* Oxford: OUP, 2006.

Klages, Mary. *Literary Theory: A Guide for the Perplexed.* London: Continuum, 2006.

Leitch, Vincent B. *The Norton Anthology of Theory & Criticism*, ed. Vincent B. Leitch. New York and London: Norton, 2010.

Makaryk, Irena R., ed. *Encyclopedia of Contemporary Literary Theory: Approaches, Scholars, Terms*. Toronto: University of Toronto Press, 1995.

Newton, K.M. *Twentieth-Century Literary Theory. A Reader.* Houndmills: Macmillan, ²1997.

Rivkin, Julie and Michael Ryan. *Literary Theory: An Anthology.* London: Blackwell, 2004.

Selden, Raman, Peter Brooker, and Peter Widdowson. *A Reader's Guide to Contemporary Literary Theory.* Lexington: Kentucky UP, 2005.

## Bibliographies and Databases (Ch. 3.8.6)

Access to these databases is provided by your local library.

- *ABELL* (= *Annual Bibliography of English Language and Literature*). The Modern Humanities Research Association.
- *American Book Publishing Record*. New York: Bowker.
- *AES* (= *Abstracts of English Studies*)
- *AHL* (= *America: History and Life*)
- *BLLDB* (= *Bibliography of Linguistic Literature DataBase*)
- *British National Bibliography*. London: Council of the British National Bibliography.
- *Cambridge Bibliography of English Literature*. Ed. Joanne Shattock.
- *MLA* (= *Modern Language Association*) *International Bibliography of Books and Articles on the Modern Languages and Literatures*. New York: MLA.
- *YWES* (= *The Year's Work in English Studies*). Ed. William Baker, Kenneth Womack. Oxford: UP, 1921-. Oxford Journals. Web. 27 July 2019. <http://ywes.oxfordjournals.org/>.[3]

### JSTOR
This digital library can be accessed by your local library (most items can be read online infinitely, be downloaded as PDF files and printed) or an individual *Register & Read*-account (you can read up to three titles for two weeks, no PDF download or printing).
<http://www.jstor.org/>.

### Project Muse
<http://muse.jhu.edu/>.

---

[3]   "*The Year's Work in English Studies* does not merely offer annotated or enumerated bibliography entries, but provides expert, critical commentary supplied for every book covered".

## Stanford Encyclopedia of Philosophy
<https://plato.stanford.edu/>.

## Questia Online Library
<http://www.questia.com/publicdomainindex>.

## Times Literary Supplement Historical Archive
<http://gale.cengage.co.uk/tls-historical-archive-19022005.aspx>.

## Voice of the Shuttle (VoS) – Literature in English
Main: <http://vos.ucsb.edu/>
English Literature: <http://vos.ucsb.edu/browse.asp?id=3>.


## Academic Writing, Language and Style Guides (Ch. 3.8.7)

### MLA Style und Chicago Style
Gibaldi, Joseph. *MLA Handbook for Writers of Research Papers.* New York: MLA, [7]2009.

Russell, Tony, Allen Brizee, Elizabeth Angeli, Russell Keck. "MLA Formatting and Style Guide". *Purdue Online Writing Lab*. 1995-2011. Web. 16 April 2019.<https://owl.purdue.edu/owl/research_and_citation/mla_style/mla_formatting_and_style_guide/mla_formatting_and_style_guide.html>.

Turabian, Kate L. *A Manual for Writers of Research Papers, Theses, and Dissertations: Chicago Style for Students and Researchers*. Chicago: University of Chicago Press, 2007.


### Plagiarism Resources, University of Fairfield

<https://librarybestbets.fairfield.edu/c.php?g=497283&p=3408643>.

## Writing and Style Guides

Bolker, Joan. *Writing Your Dissertation in 15 Minutes a Day*. New York: Holt, 1998.

Siepmann, Dirk and John D. Gallagher, Mike Hannay, Lachlan Mackenzie. *Writing in English: A Guide for Advanced Learners*. Tübingen: Francke, 2011.

Smith, Ken. *Junk English*. New York: Blast, 2001.

Strunk, William and E.B. White. *The Elements of Style*. North York, ON: General, 2019.

Walsh, Bill. *The Elephants of Style*. New York: McGraw-Hill, 2004.

Zinsser, William. *On Writing Well*. New York: Harper, 2016.

## Language

Summers, Della (ed.). *Longman Language Activator*. London: Pearson/Longman, 2004.

Swan, Michael. *Practical English Usage*. Berlin: Cornelsen, ⁴2017.